THE CATHOLIC UNIVERSITY OF AMERICA
CANON LAW STUDIES
Number 59

STOLE FEES

A DISSERTATION

Submitted to the Faculty of Canon Law of the Catholic University of America in Partial Fulfillment of the Requirements for the Degree of

DOCTOR OF CANON LAW

BY

WILLIAM A. FERRY, A.B., J.C.L.
Priest of the Archdiocese of Philadelphia

THE CATHOLIC UNIVERSITY OF AMERICA
WASHINGTON, D. C.
1930

Nihil Obstat:

PHILIPPUS BERNARDINI, S.T.D., J.U.D.,
Censor Deputatus.
Washingtonii, D. C., die V Maii, 1930.

Imprimatur:

✠ D. CARD. DOUGHERTY,
Archiepiscopus Philadelphiensis.
Philadelphiae, die VIII Maii, 1930.

COMPOSED BY
MONOTYPE COMPOSITION CO., INC.
BALTIMORE, MD.

TABLE OF CONTENTS

PART II

Canonical Aspect

BIBLIOGRAPHY

SOURCES

Acta Apostolicae Sedis (*AAS*), Romae, 1909.

Acta et Decreta Concilii Plenarii Baltimorensis II, Baltimoriae, 1868.

Acta et Decreta Concilii Plenarii Baltimorensis III, Baltimoriae, 1886.

Acta Sanctae Sedis (*ASS*), 41 vols., Romae, 1865-1908.

Bullarium Diplomatum et Privilegiorum Sanctorum Romanorum Pontificum, 24 vols., Augustae Taurinorum, 1860.

Codex Iuris Canonici, Romae, 1918.

Codicis Iuris Canonici Fontes, 4 vols., Romae, 1923-1926.

Corpus Iuris Canonici, 2 vols., Lipsiae, 1922.

Corpus Iuris Civilis, Berolini, 1922.

Mansi, Joannes, *Sacrorum Conciliorum Nova et Amplissima Collectio*, 51 vols., Parisiis, 1902-1919.

Rituale Romanum.

Thesaurus Resolutionum Sacrae Congregationis Concilii, 167 vols., Romae, 1718-1908.

AUTHORITIES

Aertnys, Jos., *Theologia Moralis*, 2 vols., Taurinorum Augustae, 1928.

Alphonsus de Ligorio, S., *Theologia Moralis*, 3 vols., Bassani, 1847.

Aquinas, Thomas, *Opera Omnia*, 34 vols., Parisiis, 1871-1880.

Ansillon, Joannes, *De Simonia et Munerum ac Retributionum Gratificatione in Re Beneficiaria*, Leodii, 1677.

Augustine, P. Charles, *A Commentary on the New Code of Canon Law*, 8 vols., New York, 1919.

Ayrinhac, H. A., *The Constitution of the Church in the New Code of Canon Law*, New York, 1925.

Ballerini, A., *Opus Theologicum Morale*, Edidit D. Palmieri, Prati, 1891.

Barbosa, A., *De Officio et Potestate Parochi, Romae*, 1774.

Barbosa, A., *Pastoralis Sollicitudinis, sive De Officio et Potestate Episcopi Tripartita Descriptio*, Lugduni, 1628.

Bargilliat, C., *Droits et Devoirs des Curés et des Vicaires paroissiaux*, 7 ed., Paris, 1919.

Bargilliat, M., *Praelectiones Juris Canonici*, 37 ed., 2 vols., Parisiis, 1923.

Benedict XIV, *Institutiones Ecclesiasticae*, Prati, 1844.
Benedict XIV, *Opera Omnia*, 12 vols., Romae, 1748.
Berardi, A., *De Parocho Compendium*, Faventiae, 1887.
Berlendi, F., *Delle Obblazioni all' Altare*, Venezia, 1736.
Bingham, Joseph, *The Antiquities of the Christian Church*, 2 vols., London, 1856.
Blat, Albertus, *Commentarium Textus Codicis Iuris Canonici*, 6 vols., Romae, 1921-1927.
Blunt, J. H., *The Book of Church Law of the Church of England*, New York, 1921.
Bonal, A., *Institutiones Canonicae*, Parisiis, 1896.
Bouix, D., *Tractatus de Parocho*, Parisiis, 1855.
Cappello, F. M., *Tractatus Canonico-moralis de Sacramentis*, 3 vols., Romae, 1927.
Cappello, F. M., *De Visitatione SS. Liminum et Dioeceseon*, 2 vols., Romae, 1913.
Carriere, Jos., *De Justitia et Jure*, 2 vols., Parisiis, 1839.
Catholic Encyclopedia, 16 vols., New York, 1907-1914.
Chelodi, Joannes, *Ius Matrimoniale*, 3 ed., Tridenti, 1921.
Cocchi, Guidus, *Commentarium in Codicem Juris Canonici*, 7 vols., Taurinorum Augustae, 1925.
Cornelius a Lapide, *Commentarium in Epistolas Canonicas*, Venetiis, 1717.
Coronata, P. M., *De Locis et Temporibus Sacris*, Augustae Taurinorum, 1922.
Cutts, E. L., *Parish Priests and Their People in the Middle Ages in England*, London, 1898.
De Luca, Card. Joan. B., *Theatrum Veritatis et Justitiae*, 16 vols., Coloniae Agrippinae, 1706.
De Meester, A., *Iuris Canonici et Iuris Canonico-Civilis Compendium*, 3 vols., Brugis, 1921-1928.
Denzinger-Bannwart, *Enchiridion Symbolorum, Definitionum et Declarationum*, 14 & 15 ed., Friburgi Brisgoviae, 1922.
De Smet, A., *Betrothment and Marriage*, 2 ed., 2 vols., Bruges, 1923.
Devoti, Joannes, *Institutionum Canonicarum Libri IV*, Leodii, 1860.
Engel, P. L., *Collegium Universi Juris Canonici*, Beneventi, 1760.
Fanfani, P. L., *De Jure Parochorum ad Normam Codicis Juris Canonici*, Taurini, 1924.
Farren, Neil, *Domicile and Quasi-domicile*, Dublin, 1920.
Farrugia, P. N., *De Matrimonio et Causis Matrimonialibus*, Taurini-Romae, 1924.
Ferraris, L. F., *Prompta Bibliotheca Canonica*, Parisiis, 1865.
Funk, F. X., *Manual of Church History*, St. Louis, 1910.
Gardellini, Aloisius, *Decreta Authentica Congregationis Sacrorum Rituum*, 3 ed., Romae, 1856.

Gasparri, P., *Tractatus Canonicus de SS. Eucharistia,* 2 vols., Parisiis, 1897.

Gasquet, Abbot, *Parish Life in Mediaeval England,* New York, 1906.

Genicot, E., *Institutiones Theologiae Moralis,* 10 ed., 2 vols., Bruxellis, 1922.

Gibalini, Jos., *De Simonia Universa Tractatio Theologica et Canonica,* Lugduni, 1659.

Giraldi, U., *Additiones et Animadversiones ad Barbosa De Officio et Potestate Parochi,* Romae, 1831.

Golden, H. F., *Parochial Benefices in the New Code,* Washington, 1921.

Guy, Robt. E., *The Synods in English,* Stratford-on-Avon, 1886.

Johnson, John, *A Collection of the Laws and Canons of the Church of England,* Oxford, 1850.

Keller, C. F., *Mass Stipends,* Washington, 1925.

Laymann, Paul, *Theologia Moralis,* Venetiis, 1719.

Leage, R. W., *Roman Private Law,* London, 1924.

Lesetre, *La Paroisse,* Paris, 1908.

Lingard, John, *The History and Antiquities of the Anglo Saxon Church,* London, 1845.

Lingen and Reuss, *Causae Selectae in S. Congregatione Cardinalium Concilii Tridentini Interpretum Propositae,* Ratisbonae, 1871.

Lowrie, Walter, *The Church and Its Organization in Primitive and Catholic Times,* New York, 1904.

Many, S., *Praelectiones de Locis Sacris,* Parisiis, 1904.

Maroto, P., *Institutiones Juris Canonici,* 3 ed., 2 vols., Romae, 1921.

Migne, P. J., *Patrologiae Graecae Cursus Completus* (*MPG*), Parisiis, 1856-1864.

Migne, P. J., *Patrologia Latina* (*MPL*), Parisiis, 1847-1851.

Mostazo, F., *Tractatus de Causis Piis,* 2 vols., Venetiis, 1715.

Ojetti, Bened., *Synopsis Rerum Moralium et Juris Pontificii,* 3 ed., 3 vols., Romae, 1911.

Pallotini, S., *Collectio omnium conclusionum et resolutionum quae in causis propositis apud Sacram Congregationem Cardinalium S. Concilii Tridentini interpretum prodierunt,* 17 vols., Romae, 1887.

Pastor, Melchior, *Liber de Bonis Temporalibus Ecclesiae,* Tolosae, 1675.

Petavius, Dionysius, *Dogmata Theologica,* 8 vols., Parisiis, 1867.

Pichler, R. P. V., *Epitome Juris Canonici,* Venetiis, 1755.

Pirhing, P. E., *Jus Canonicum,* Dilingae, 1678.

Reiffenstuel, Anacletus, *Ius Canonicum Universum,* 4 vols., Venetiis, 1735.

Rossi, Jos., *De Matrimonii Celebratione,* Romae, 1924.

Rossi, G., *La "Sepultura Ecclesiastica," e l' "Ius Funerum" nel Diritto Canonico,* Bergamo, 1920.

Santi, Franciscus, *Praelectiones Iuris Canonici,* 2 vols., Ratisbon, 1892.
Schmalzgrueber, F., *Ius Ecclesiasticum Universum,* 12 vols., Romae, 1843-1845.
Smith, S. B., *Counter-points in Canon Law,* Newark, 1879.
Smith, S. B., *Elements of Ecclesiastical Law,* 4 ed., New York, 1881.
Smith, S. B., *Notes on the Second Plenary Council of Baltimore,* New York, 1874.
Soglia, Joannes, *Institutiones Juris Privati Ecclesiastici,* 2 ed., 3 vols., Parisiis, 1854.
Solier, Joannes, *Addita ad Pastor Liber de Bonis Temporalibus Ecclesiae,* Tolosae, 1675.
Thiel, A., *Epistolae Romanorum Pontificum Genuinae,* Brunsbergae, 1868.
Thomassinus, Ludovicus, *Vetus et Nova Ecclesiae Disciplina,* 3 vols., Magontiaci, 1787.
Ugolinus, Bartholomeus, *Tractatus de Simonia,* Venetiis, 1599.
Vecchiotti, S. M., *Institutiones Canonicae,* 10 ed., 3 vols., *Augustae Taurinorum,* 1886.
Vermeersch-Creusen, *Epitome Iuris Canonici,* 3 ed., 3 vols., Mechliniae, 1927.
Vlaming, Th. M., *Praelectiones Iuris Matrimonii,* 3 ed., 2 vols., Bussum, 1919-1921.
Vogt, Jos., *Das kirchliche Vermögensrecht,* 2 ed., Cologne, 1910.
Vromant, G., *De Bonis Ecclesiae temporalibus,* Louvain, 1927.
Weber, N. A., *A History of Simony in the Christian Church,* Baltimore, 1909.
Wernz, F. X., *Jus Decretalium,* Prati, 1915.
Wernz-Vidal, *Jus Canonicum,* 3 vols., Romae, 1923-1927.
Westermarck, Edward, *The History of Human Marriage,* London, 1891.
Woywod, Stanislaus, *A Practical Commentary on the Code of Canon Law,* 2 vols., New York, 1926.

PERIODICALS

American Ecclesiastical Review, Philadelphia, 1889-
Apollinaris, Romae, 1928-
Canoniste Contemporain, Le, Paris, 1878-
Collationes Brugenses, Bruges, 1896-
Irish Ecclesiastical Record, Dublin, 1897-
Ius Pontificium, Romae, 1921-
Nineteenth Century, The, New York, 1877-
Nouvelle Revue Théologique, Paris, 1856-
Periodica de Re Canonica et Morali, Romae et Brugis, 1905-

FOREWORD

Although there are undoubtedly many questions of greater importance in the field of Canon Law, the subject of stole fees has much to recommend it as a topic for research and commentary. The numerous cases and queries propounded for solution to the editors of the various ecclesiastical periodicals are an evidence that it is not without interest to the clergy. They are at the same time an indication that in formulating the canons of the New Code which refer to stole fees, the legislator has sacrificed something of clarity to conciseness. For the most part, commentators on the New Code of Canon Law give but meagre attention to this subject, reserving and directing their lore and study to other, more important questions; very often they do no more than repeat, rearrange or translate the text of the law. Of the few works written professedly on stole fees that have come to the present writer's attention,[1] none is in English, all antedate the New Code—which introduced some modifications of the former law, and all are out of print and difficult to obtain. These facts seemed more than sufficient to justify it as the topic of a doctorate dissertation.

A word of explanation is necessary by way of apology for the historical survey in the early pages, lest this appear to be a tedious and meticulous investigation into trifles. Among the canons for interpretation, the Code [2] states that to determine the meaning of doubtful and obscure laws, recourse must be had to the purpose of the law and the circumstances surrounding it, and to the mind of the lawgiver. It is manifest, however, that for the better under-

[1] Grellman, *Geschichte der Stolgebühren*, 1785. Riedle, *Das Pfarramtliche Recht der Stolgebühren*, München, 1897. Palacin, Alonso, *Defensa y Reivindicacion de los Derechos de Estola y Pie de Altar*, Soria, 1914.

[2] Can. 18.

standing of any law, the prescriptions given to determine those which are doubtful and obscure still obtain. For this reason it seemed advisable, before commenting on the canonical legislation regulating stole fees, to institute an inquiry into their origin, and to trace, as far as possible, their historical evolution and development by a review of past legislation on the subject and the causes which gave rise to it.

The writer desires to express his gratitude to the Faculty of Canon Law for their advice and encouragement with this dissertation. He is also indebted to Rev. Joseph La Rue, Rev. Mark Ebner and Rev. Donald Gregory for their generous assistance in preparing it for the printer.

PART I

Historical Development

CHAPTER I

Pious Offerings

The practice of making oblations which the Jews observed towards the priests of the Old Law was more than a regulation of the ancient Synagogue; it was a shadow and a figure of a custom in the Church of the Messiah,[1] by which the faithful, prompted by piety and gratitude towards God, contribute to His representatives, the priests of the New Dispensation. "With God, there is nothing vain, nothing without a sign and a reason . . . Wherefore (God) wishes us also to offer gifts to the altar often and without intermission. For there is an altar in the heavens, and thither our prayers and our oblations are directed." [2]

The generic term "oblation" comprehends whatever is freely offered to God and the Church by the faithful.[3] Oblations have been variously classified, most authors adhering to a threefold division substantially similar to Devoti's analysis which, for the sake of clarity, is employed here.[4] The latter places in the first class all those oblations which were used in offering sacrifice, such as bread and wine for the Eucharist, milk and honey for baptism, and

---

[1] Berlendi, *Delle Obblazioni all'Altare*, Parte I, §1, I.

[2] Irenaeus, *Adv. Haeres.*, Lib. IV, cap. 18, nn. 2 & 6 (*MPG*, VII, 1025 & 1029).

[3] Devoti, *Inst. Canon.*, Lib. II, tit. XVII, §III; Solier, Additio ad Pastoris opus, *Liber de Bonis Temp. Eccl.*, Tit. III (a); *Capitularia Caroli Magni*, Lib. VI, c. 407 (Mansi, XVII^{B}, 1002*-*1003).

[4] Devoti, *l. c.*, Lib. II, tit. XVII, §§IV, V, & VI; Berlendi, *l. c.*; Soglia, *Inst. Jur. Priv. Eccl.*, Lib. II, cap. I, n. 73.

so on; free-will offerings constitute the second class, whether these were for the maintenance of the church or for the sustentation of the clergy and the poor; the third division comprises all those donations that were made to the clergy on the occasion of funerals, the administration of the Sacraments and other sacerdotal functions. It is with the oblations which fall under the last classification that we are here concerned. Originally voluntary, these offerings gradually received the approval of legitimate custom and the sanction of law;[5] thenceforth they were of obligation, and the faithful were no longer free to observe them or not, the bishops being empowered by Innocent III to compel obedience to a custom introduced by Christian piety.[6]

Stole fees, then, are the offerings made to the minister on the occasion of certain priestly functions. They derive their name from the fact that the minister usually wears a stole at the ceremonies to which such offerings are attached.[7] The pastor's rights to receive such fees are territorial, personal and exclusive,[8] that is to say, within the limits of his own parish, he alone is juridically entitled to these offerings from the faithful who reside in that territory.

These rights are not the mushroom growth of a century; rather, they are fortified by venerable traditions and the legal sanction of a millenium. Unfortunately, however, treatment of the historical aspect of stole fees offers difficulty because there is no definite and uniform starting place for the various phases of the subject. One difficulty is presented by the fact that parishes and pastors, as they are now, had chronologically different origins. Then, too,

---

[5] Soglia, *Inst. Jur. Priv. Eccl.*, Lib. II, cap. I, n. 73, 3; Ayrinhac, *Constitution of the Church*, n. 271; Devoti, *Inst. Canon.*, Lib. II, tit. XVII, §VI; Vogt, *Das kirchliche Vermögensrecht*, §39, 1.

[6] IV Lateran C., c. 66 (Mansi, XXII, 1054).

[7] Ojetti, *Synopsis*, v. *Jura Stolae*, n. 2254.

[8] Wernz-Vidal, *Jus Canonicum*, I, n. 731.

the functions to which stole fees are attached, and at which the pastor has an exclusive right to officiate, were not always performed by him; the right to assist at some of them he acquired gradually by concession of the Bishop, to whom they were originally reserved.[9] Finally, the pastor had not always the right to administer the revenues of his own parish, from whatever source they proceeded.

It would be absurd to ignore these facts, and illogical to defer treatment of them, since they antedate the other aspects of stole fees. Therefore, before developing the historical defense of the rights of pastors mentioned above, it is proposed to outline briefly the origin of pastors, parishes and parochial functions, and to make some slight comment on the ancient administration of revenues.

Article I.—Preliminary Remarks

§1. *The Origin of Parishes.*—Most authorities declare that there were no parishes during the first three centuries of the Christian era, basing their assertion on the argument of silence on the part of ecclesiastical writers of this period.[10] There was but one church in a diocese at which all the faithful attended.[11] This was the Cathedral Church where the Bishop presided,[12] and he was immediately responsible for the spiritual welfare of his flock.[13]

The fourth century saw the rise of the parochial system. The increasing number of the faithful [14] in cities like

---

[9] Thomassin, *Vet. et Nov. Eccl. Disciplina,* Pars I, lib. II, cap. XXIII, §17.

[10] Thomassin, *Vet. et Nov. Eccl. Discipl.,* Pars I, lib. II, cap. XXI, §§1-4; Devoti, *Inst. Canon.,* Lib. I, tit. III, sect. X, LXXXVII; Smith, *Elements of Ecclesiastical Law,* n. 639, 2; Wernz, *Jus Decretalium,* II, §84, III.

[11] S. Justin M., *Apol.* 1, No. 67 (*MPG,* VI, 430-431).

[12] Devoti, *Inst. Canon.,* Lib. I, tit. III, sect. X, LXXXVII; Thomassin, *Eccl. Discipl.,* Pars I, lib. II, cap. XXI, §4.

[13] *Canon. Apost.,* c. 40 (Mansi, I, 55).

[14] Soglia, *Inst. Jur. Priv. Eccl.,* Lib. I, cap. II, No. 25; Devoti, *l. c.*

Rome[15] and Alexandria[16] necessitated the formation of parishes to care for them. With the spread of the faith in the country districts and villages, the inaccessibility of the church for the faithful, together with the difficulty and inconvenience of ministering to such a scattered flock compelled the bishops to have recourse to the same expedient.[17] From this time on, ecclesiastical writers and councils make frequent references to parishes in rural districts.[18] But with the exception of Rome, Alexandria and perhaps one or two other great cities, the formation of city parishes did not take place till about the year 1000.[19]

§2. *The Clergy of the Early Parishes.*—It was some time after the establishment of parishes before the parochial clergy became stable and fixed. This was true at least of the parishes in large cities. Whatever mention ancient documents make concerning rural parishes seems to indicate that they were served by fixed clergy from a very early date,[20] if not from the beginning. City parishes, on the other hand, were at first administered by the cathedral clergy, who took turns in officiating in them on Sundays.[21] This practice obtained in Constantinople at least till the time of Justinian,[22] who mentions several churches in that

---

[15] Thomassin, *op. cit.*, Pars I, lib. II, cap. XXI, §11; Devoti, *l. c.*, footnote (1); *Liber Pontificale*, in vita Dionysii P. (Mansi, I, 1003) mentions parishes in Rome, but Soglia (*l. c.*) asserts that the canon by which Dionysius established parishes in Rome is called apocryphal by many; *Lib. Pontif.*, in vita Marcelli P. (Mansi, I, 1259) asserts that Marcellus founded twenty-five.

[16] Mentioned by Epiphanius, *Adv. Haeres.*, *LXVIII*, No. 4 (*MPG*, XLII, 190-191) & LXIX, No. 1 (*MPG*, XLII, 202-203); Athanasius, *Apol. contra Arianos*, §85 (*MPG*, XXV, 399).

[17] Devoti, *op. cit.*, Lib. I, tit. III, sect. X, LXXXIX; Thomassin, *op. cit.*, Pars I, lib. II, cap. XXII, §§3 & 10; Bingham, *Antiquities*, Bk. IX, ch. VIII, sect. I; Soglia, *l. c.*

[18] Innocent I, *Ep. I ad Decentium*, c. 5 (Mansi, III, 1030); C. Sardica, 347, c. 6 (Mansi, III, 10); C. Vaison, 442, c. 2 (Mansi VI, 453); C. Chalcedon, 451, c. 17 (Mansi, VII, 397).

[19] Bergomensis, *De Paroch. Ante An. Xti. Milles.* (quoted from Devoti, *Inst. Canon.*, Lib. I, tit. III, sect. X, LXXXVII, footnote (1)).

[20] Bingham, *Antiquities*, Bk. IX, ch. VIII, sect. 6.

[21] Devoti, *op. cit.*, Lib. I, tit. III, sect. X, LXXXVIII; Bingham, *l. c.*

[22] Bingham, *l. c.*

metropolis which had no appropriated clergy attached to them, but were served in courses by the priests of the cathedral church.[23]

Most authors declare that Alexandria was an exception to this custom,[24] and base their arguments on textual criticism of a passage in Epiphanius,[25] who seems to speak of fixed clergy as peculiar to Alexandria. Whether Rome had fixed clergy at the time Innocent I wrote to Decentius[26] is controverted. Valesius[27] denies this, while Petavius[28] thinks that the clergy of all great cities were fixed.

§3. *Appropriation of Parochial Revenues.*—The ancient method of administering the revenues of a diocese required that all the oblations of the various parishes be forwarded to the bishop for distribution.[29] It was customary to divide these revenues into four parts, one for the bishop, one for the clergy, one to be distributed among the poor, and one for the maintenance and repair of church property.[30] This division was not necessitated where the clergy lived a community life with their bishop, as was the custom with St. Augustine;[31] elsewhere it was monthly or annually as custom decreed.[32]

---

[23] Novel. 3, c. 1.

[24] Devoti, *Inst. Canon.*, Lib. I, tit. III, sect. X, LXXXVIII; Bingham, *Antiquities*, Bk. IX, ch. VIII, sect. 6.

[25] *Adv. Haeres.*, LXIX, No. 1 (*MPG*, XLII, 202-203).

[26] *Ep. I ad Decent., Episc. Eugubin.*, 416, c. 5 (Mansi, III, 1030).

[27] Adnotatio (59) in Sozomen, *Hist. Eccl.*, Lib. I, c. 15 (*MPG*, LXVII, 907-910).

[28] *De Eccl. Hierarchia*, Lib. II, cap. 12 (*Theol. Dogmat.*, VII, p. 633).

[29] *Canones Apost.*, c. 40 (Mansi, I, 38); *Const. Apost.*, Lib. II, c. 25 (Mansi, I, 323).

[30] Gregory I, *Response to Augustine*, cap. I (Mansi, X, 415): "*Mos enim Sedis Apostolicae est, ut . . . IV debeant fieri portiones; una videlicet Episcopo, . . . alia clero, tertia pauperibus, quarta ecclesiis reparandis . . .*"; C. Treves, 895, can. 13 (Mansi, XVIIIA, 140).

[31] Augustine, *Sermon 357* (*II De Vit. et Mor. Cler.*), §13 (*MPL*, XXXIX, 1579-1580); Possidius, *Vita Augustin.*, cap. 25 (*MPL*, XXXII, 54-55).

[32] Bingham, *Antiquities*, Bk. IX, ch. VIII, sect. 6.

For some centuries, therefore, the "being settled in a parish-cure did not entitle a man to the revenue arising from that cure, whether in tithes or oblations, or any other kind," [33] a fact which is evident from a comparison of the dates when fixed clergy are found and those of the assigning of its proper revenue to each parish. The appropriation of parish income to its proper church was necessitated by the multiplication of parishes and of contributions in kind,[34] and the difficulty and inconvenience of making a just distribution.

The custom of a common fund obtained in Constantinople, at least until the middle of the fifth century, when Marcion, the economus or administrator of church income, ordered a church to appropriate its revenue to its own use.[35] In Spain, the appropriation of revenues to their proper churches was effected by the Third Council of Braca,[36] which directed bishops to refrain from sharing in the oblations of parochial churches,[37] allowing them to receive only the cathedraticum. In Germany and France the change did not take place till a much later date,[38] and Gasquet [39] declares that, although tithes were administered by the local parson when parishes were firmly established in England,[40] the fundamental idea underlying them until the time of the Reformation was that the fourfold division should be made.

§4. *Development of Sacerdotal Functions.*—During the first three centuries of the Church Baptism was ordinarily conferred by the Bishop; he alone administered the sacrament of Penance, and he alone offered the sacrifice of the

---

[33] Bingham, *l. c.*

[34] Ayrinhac, *Constitution of the Church*, n. 271, 1.

[35] Theodore Lector, Lib. I, 15 (*MPG*, LXXXVIII, 171 & 174).

[36] 572, can. 2 (Mansi, IX, 839).

[37] Bingham (*Antiquities*, Bk. IX, ch. VIII, sect. 6), applies this to "country parishes."

[38] Bingham, *l. c.*

[39] *Parish Life in Mediæval England*, p. 18.

[40] Cutts (*Parish Priests and Their People in the Middle Ages in England*, p. 46), attributes diocesan and parochial organization to Theodore (668-690).

Mass unless he chose one of his priests to substitute for him as celebrant.[41] He was immediately responsible for the spiritual care of the faithful, and the priests who assisted him were forbidden to administer Baptism or to celebrate the Eucharist without his permission.[42] In his Epistle to Polycarp,[43] Ignatius indicates that it was the Bishop likewise who assisted at the celebration of Matrimony. There is reason to believe that the Oriental clergy enjoyed no more ample faculties in this regard than the priests of the Western Church. Certainly this was true of conferring the more solemn form of Baptism, which was reserved to the Bishop, unless he were absent or a case of urgent necessity arose.[44] This restriction probably obtained in the Orient at least till the early fifth century; although several of the Apostolic Canons [45] mention the Bishop and the priest indiscriminately as the minister of Baptism, a previous one [46] declares explicitly that priests and deacons are to consult their Bishop about everything that pertains to their flock and to do nothing without advising him.

Concessions had evidently been made in favor of the clergy of the Western Church towards the close of the fourth century. The Fourth Council of Carthage [47] speaks of priests as imparting the nuptial blessing. They were no longer restricted to cases of necessity in administering Baptism,[48] and towards the middle of the fifth century they were permitted to bless the families, fields and homes of the faithful.[49]

---

[41] Thomassin, *Vetus et Nova Eccl. Discipl.,* Pars I, lib. II, cap. XXI, §8 & cap. XXIII, §3.

[42] Ignatius, *Ep. ad Smyrnaeos,* cap. VIII (*MPG,* V, 714); Tertulian, *De Bapt.,* cap. 17 (*MPL,* I, 1218, A).

[43] Cap. V (*MPG,* V, 723).

[44] Thomassin, *op. cit.,* Pars I, lib. II, cap. XXIII, §14.

[45] Cans. 46, 48 & 49 (Mansi, I, 39, B & C).

[46] Can. 38 (Mansi I, 38, B).

[47] 398, can. 13 (Mansi, III, 952, C); c. 33, D. XXIII.

[48] Innocent I, *Ep. I ad Decent.,* Episc. Eugubin., 19 Mar. 416 (Mansi, III, 1029, C).

[49] C. Reggio, 439, can. 5 (Mansi, V, 1093, C).

As late as the sixth and seventh centuries, the old discipline by which ecclesiastical functions were reserved to the Bishop when he was present perdured in most places; it was gradually relaxing, however, due to the fact that the faithful were increasing to such extent that it was impossible for the Bishops to minister to all personally.[50] The inconvenience of reaching parishes remote from the Episcopal seat tended to accelerate this relaxation in the rural districts, so that priests in such territory enjoyed greater jurisdiction than those whose parishes were easily accessible to the Bishop; even at this time, however, it was not unusual for a priest or a deacon to confer Baptism in the presence of the Bishop.[51]

A canon of the Second Council of Aix-le-Chapelle [52] offers some idea of the duties of the priestly office in the early ninth century: the pastor is to preach, to teach, to correct the erring, to console the sick and fortify them with Extreme Unction and Viaticum, and to see that the dead receive Christian burial. From this time on, the canons against exactions on the occasion of ecclesiastical ceremonies are a sufficient indication that there was practically universal and unrestricted exercise of the functions of the priestly office.

§5. *Laws against Promiscuous Ministration.*—Since the parochial system was invented to care for the spiritual necessities of the faithful, it was only just and right that they should be compelled to attend the church assigned to them. Especially was this expedient when parishes were assigned their proper revenues, and the clergy could no longer depend on the common fund but must needs subsist on the generosity of the faithful within their district. That the ecclesiastical authorities fully realized this is abundantly evidenced by the records of legislation on the subject.

At the outset there is a canon that appears to militate against this assertion. About the middle of the eighth cen-

---

[50] Thomassin, *Vet. et Nov. Eccl. Discipl.*, Pars I, lib. II, cap. XXIII, §17.

[51] Thomassin, *op. cit.*, Pars I, lib. II, cap. XXIII, §§2 & 18.

[52] 836, can. 5 (Mansi, XIV, 680-681).

tury in England Lord Ecgbright decreed: "Let priests give the sacrament of baptism promiscuously to all that want it; . . ."[53] But this objection is sufficiently solved by the fact that parishes were not introduced into England till the end of the seventh century,[54] and it was not till the following century that their proper revenues were settled upon them.[55] About the time of Charlemagne, however, the law of tithes and oblations was gradually acquiring recognition, and it would have been unjust to permit the faithful to satisfy these obligations otherwise than to the pastor who ministered to their wants.[56]

Herardus, Archbishop of Tours,[57] forbade his priests to solicit or receive the parishioners of another pastor unless they were excused by reason of a journey or had the permission of their proper pastor. A Council held towards the end of the ninth century[58] directed parish priests to inquire before Mass on Sundays and Feasts if there were any strangers present, and if so, to compel them to attend their own church. One of King Edgar's laws[59] forbade priests to interfere in the parochial rights of another pastor, and the "Book of Church Laws"[60] condemned those who solicited the parishioners of another, or who induced them to pay to themselves the tithes and rights which belonged to another, directing each to be satisfied with what came to him from his own church.

In the year 1102, Anselm, Archbishop of Canterbury, in a synod held at Westminster,[61] directed that corpses should not be buried outside their proper parishes, to the financial

---

53 *Excerpts of Lord Ecgbright*, No. 40 (Mansi, XII, 417).

54 Cutts, *Parish Priests and Their People in the Middle Ages in England*, p. 46.

55 Bingham, *Antiquities*, Bk. IX, ch. VIII, §4.

56 Thomassin, *Vet. et Nov. Eccl. Discipl.*, Pars I, lib. II, cap. XXIV, §5.

57 *Capitularies of Herardus*, c. 29 (Mansi, XVII^{B}, *1287).

58 C. Nancy, c. 1 (Mansi, XVIII^{A}, 166).

59 *Leges Eccl. Reg. Edgardi*, c. 9 (Mansi, XVIII^{A}, 514).

60 994, c. 14 (Mansi, XIX, 183); Johnson (*English Canons*, 994, 14) calls it "Theodulf's Capitula" and interprets it as above.

61 C. London, c. 25 (Mansi, XX, 1152).

prejudice of their pastors. Previous laws had required that a mortuary, called the "soul-scot," be paid to the proper pastor of the deceased in such instances.[62]

Officiating at the marriage service of any but one's own parishioners, except with the proper permission, was severely punished by Archbishop Stratford: ". . . priests who knowingly make solemnization of . . . marriages . . . between such as do not belong to their parishes (without first having obtained the license of their diocesans, or of the curates of the parties contracting), . . . do incur the sentence of excommunication, ipso facto; . . ."[63]

In case of spiritual necessity, however, the rigor of the law was not pressed. Priests were not only permitted, but commanded under pain of deposition, to baptize and to administer the last sacraments to those in danger of death, irrespective of whether they had jurisdiction over them or not.[64]

Article II.—The Theory of Stole Fees

§1. *The Reason for Stole Fees.*—Saint Ambrose[65] taught that the "sacraments are so precious that they may be given; but they can neither be bought nor sold; for they are graces, not merchandise: or rather they are heavenly merchandise, which can be acquired only with supernatural virtues." The faithful have always realized this, and there was never a misunderstanding on their part, by which they were led to believe that their oblation was the price of the priestly ministration.[66] The donation was made as an ac-

[62] C. Eanham, 1009, Tit. "De Censu Lumin. et Sepult," (Mansi, XIX, 301); *Cnute's Ecclesiastical Laws*, 1032, c. 13 (Mansi, XIX, 558).

[63] C. London, 1342, can. 11 (Mansi XXV, 1177-1178); Johnson, *English Canons*, 1343, 11.

[64] C. Chelsea, 816, c. 11 (Mansi, XIV, 360); *Liber Legum Eccl.*, 994, c. 18 (Mansi, XIX, 183-184); C. York, 1195, c. 4 (Mansi, XXII, 653-654).

[65] *In Evang. Luc.*

[66] Gasquet, *Parish Life in Mediæval England*, p. 187; Vogt, *Das kirchliche Vermögensrecht*, §39, 1.

knowledgment of special service,[67] and as tangible evidence of their recognition of the constant care for their souls which the pastor exercised,[68] and for which he was responsible. That particular ministration which was the occasion of the oblation was merely an instance of this care, an important evidence and example of unremitting solicitude for their spiritual welfare.

There is substantial proof for this assertion in the reasons adduced by practically all authorities for the so-called "funeral fourth," that portion of the funeral fees which is due to a pastor when the obsequies for one of his parishioners are conducted in another parish. They explain his right to this payment in this way: it is the pastor who pours the waters of regeneration upon his flock and confers on them spiritual life; it is through his mediation that they obtain pardon for their transgressions in the sacrament of penance; and it is he who nourishes them with the Bread of Life and the word of divine truth. For this life-long service in their behalf recognition is made with the "funeral fourth," [69] and his rights to it have been vindicated in one form or another from the time that the parochial system was once universally established.[70] Moreover, the argument of necessity compels acceptance of this explanation; there exists no other logical reason for it.

There are numerous other arguments to support the assertion that such oblations are given in recognition of the pastor's constant care and service. For instance, when a priest officiates in the church of another, he is bound to transmit any oblations made to him to the pastor of the church; and the latter is likewise entitled to the offerings made in a chapel or other church within his parish limits,[71]

---

[67] Gasquet, *op. cit.*, p. 9.

[68] Devoti, *Inst. Canon.*, Lib. II, tit. XVII, VII; Solier, Additio ad Pastoris opus, *Liber de Bonis Temp. Eccl.*, Tit. III, (b).

[69] Barbosa, *De Offic. et Potest. Episc.*, Pars III, LXXV, 46; Devoti, *Inst. Canon.*, Lib. II, tit. IX, VIII; Soglia, *Inst. Jur. Priv. Eccl.*, Lib. II, cap. IV, No. 127.

[70] See Ch. II, art. III.

[71] Solier, Additio ad Pastoris opus, *Liber de Bonis Temp. Eccl.*, Tit. III (b).

unless this be exempt from his jurisdiction. There is also the fact that the ministration is in no way dependent on the fee and cannot be refused for it;[72] and, moreover, it is noteworthy that councils which authorized exactions permitted them only *after* the ceremony, and almost invariably contained the injunction that nothing was to be exacted from those who could ill afford to give. To investigate other aspects of these offerings would further confirm the above assertion, but these facts alone would seem sufficient to justify it; at any rate, it must be admitted that there can be no question of selling the ministry in a practice which assigns the temporality to the pastor when another officiates, and this will be demonstrated more conclusively in the pages on the simoniacal aspect of stole fees.[73]

§2. *The Obligation of Offering Stole Fees.*—It is possible to justify the assertion that the faithful are under a grave obligation to support the clergy by many passages from the New Testament. In the Gospel of Matthew [74] Christ says: "The workman is worthy of his meat," and in Luke:[75] "The laborer is worthy of his hire," while Paul [76] asks: "Who planteth a vineyard, and eateth not of the fruit thereof? Who feedeth the flock, and eateth not of the milk of the flock? . . . If we have sown unto you spiritual things, is it a great matter if we reap your carnal things? . . . Know you not that they who work in the holy place, eat the things that are of the holy place; and they that serve the altar, partake with the altar? So also the Lord ordained that they who preach the gospel, should live by the gospel."

While these texts indicate that by divine law the faithful can be under an obligation to support the clergy,[77] they in no way authorize the making of oblations on the occasion of spiritual ministrations. Whatever obligation such pas-

---

[72] Vogt, *Das kirchliche Vermögensrecht*, §39, 1.

[73] See Ch. I, art. II, §4.

[74] X, 10.

[75] X, 7.

[76] I. Cor., IX, 7, 11, 13 & 14.

[77] Cornel. a Lapid., *Comment. in Sac. Scrip.*, in. I Cor., IX, 12-14.

sages impose is not sufficiently specific to justify using them as arguments to enforce the making of offerings at sacerdotal functions.

It might be argued from reason that the general obligation to support the clergy is most logically fulfilled by contributions on such occasions. Authors in general[78] admit this when the ministers would otherwise lack sufficient means to provide for their support. It is necessary, however, to advance an argument that will justify such an obligation, even in instances where the ministers derive sufficient income from other sources to care for their wants.

That argument, and the obligation itself, are derived from one source, namely, traditional and laudable custom, sanctioned by legitimate prescription or the express consent of competent authority.

§3. *Laudable Customs.*—The term "laudable custom" comprehends all those pious gifts and voluntary oblations which are wont to be offered in the administration of the sacraments, in visiting the sick, burying the dead, and on the occasion of other religious ceremonies.[79] From existing manuscripts and ancient documents it has been estimated that there were six hundred different oblations which were made by custom at various sacerdotal functions.[80] It is superfluous to add that these were not all customary in any one place. Diocesan custom is the authority that determines what ministrations shall have oblations attached to them and what not,[81] and the decrees of the various councils touching on the subject are sufficient indication that local custom has always decided this point.

It will be demonstrated later that oblations for baptism, marriage and funerals were practically universally observed, but there were other oblations peculiar to different

---

78 S. Thomas Aq., *Summa,* 2, 2, qu. 86, art. 1; Barbosa, *De Off. et Pot. Parochi,* cap. XXIV, n. 10; Bouix, *Tract. de Parocho,* Pars IV, cap. IX, §1, qu. 4, 3°.

79 Thomassin, *Vet. et Nov. Eccl. Discipl.,* Pars III, lib. I, cap. LXXII, §1.

80 Thomassin, *l. c.*

81 Vogt, *Das kirchliche Vermögensrecht,* §39, 2.

places. A provincial synod of London [82] in 1328, mentions offerings for the purification of women; and the Councils of London [83] and Westminster [84] reprobated exactions for communion, visiting the sick and anointing, in addition to the functions already noted. Time, too, played an important part in the development of these oblations. Offerings at baptism and funerals are of great antiquity, while those on the occasion of marriage were not common till centuries later.

The importance of custom in determining oblations is evident from what has been said. The nature of this custom and its binding power remain to be demonstrated.

For a custom to obtain legal force it is necessary that it be introduced without the persuasion of authority, by at least a majority of the people;[85] moreover, it must persist for at least forty years.[86] Thenceforth it is considered established and those who are bound by it and who refuse to abide by it can be compelled to do so,[87] even under pain of excommunication,[88] for in continuing the practice it is presumed that there is the intention of inducing an obligation.[89] However, there is no obligation to conform to the custom on the part of those who are unable to make an oblation.[90]

Although custom derives the force of law only from the consent of authority,[91] legitimate prescription is equivalent to such consent and establishes a custom with the same obligation as regards its observance as written law; for the legislator is interpreted to approve the custom by his

[82] Can. 7 (Mansi, XXV, 832).

[83] 1125, c. 2 (Mansi, XXI, 330).

[84] 1138, c. 1 (Mansi, XXI, 511).

[85] Ferraris, vv. *Consuetudo*, 7 & 9 and *Oblationes*, 11; Barbosa, *De Off. et Pot. Paroch.*, Pars III, cap. XXIV, 12.

[86] *Codex J. C.*, can. 28. Before the Code there were various estimates on this point, most authors contending that ten years sufficed; cf. footnote 85 supra.

[87] Barbosa, *op. cit.*, Pars III, cap. XXIV, 11.

[88] Ferraris, v. *Oblationes*, 12.

[89] Mostazo, *Tract. de Causis Piis*, Lib. IV, cap. XII, nn. 14 & 34.

[90] Barbosa, *De Offic. et Pot. Paroch.*, Pars III, cap. XXIV, 11.

[91] C. 3, D. XII; c. 9, X, *de consuet.*, I, 4.

silence,[92] just as the faithful are presumed to intend to induce an obligation by observing the custom. This may be understood, however, to refer only to reasonable customs.

How customs referring to oblations may be reasonable —prescinding from those which are juridically reprobated, which are evidently unreasonable [93]—is best explained by an illustration. The Synodal Constitutions of Odo, Bishop of Paris,[94] permitted not only that the accustomed baptismal oblation be received, but also exacted, after the ceremony, while the Council of Tours [95] expressly reprobated exactions and declared that long observance of such corruptions did not diminish but rather augmented their gravity. Thomassin [96] offers a plausible explanation of this contradiction. He says that in Tours there were probably sufficient revenues from tithes, first-fruits and other oblations to sustain the clergy, while in the City of Paris, as might be expected, there were no such sources of income and the pastors had to depend more on occasional offerings to provide for their necessities. It is evident, therefore, that in determining what is reasonable and what not, no hard and fast rule can be stated; external circumstances enter into the case to such extent that they become the determining factors, except where there is question of what is morally right and wrong.

It is difficult to determine just when offerings began to be made on the occasion of spiritual ministrations. The Apostolic Canons [97] in treating of oblations make no mention of anything that would correspond to such offerings. These Canons were written in the fourth [98] or the beginning of the fifth [99] century. It might be argued from this that there were no such offerings till the fifth century or later; but this is evidently false. Such offerings, at baptism, at

[92] Reg. Jur. XLIII, in VI°: "Qui tacet, consentire videtur."
[93] C. 2, *de consuet.*, I, 4, in VI°.
[94] 1197, cap. 3, n. 2 (Mansi, XXII, 677).
[95] 1163, c. 6 (Mansi, XXI, 1178).
[96] *Vet. et Nov. Eccl. Discipl.*, Pars III, lib. I, cap. LXXII, §4.
[97] Cans. 3, 4 & 5 (Mansi, I, 50-51).
[98] Maroto, *Inst. Jur. Can.*, I, n. 42.
[99] Funk, *Manual of Church History*, I, §75 (page 222).

any rate, were prevalent enough in Spain in the year 305 for the Council of Elvira [100] to prohibit their acceptance. If, as seems probable, they were confined to certain localities in early times, the practice of making them gradually spread. The Councils of the first eight centuries frequently prohibit their acceptance,[101] and even after that time they are occasionally reprobated.[102]

Thomassin,[103] summarizing the decrees of councils before the middle of the thirteenth century referring to laudable customs, writes:

> The canons thus far reviewed are for the most part in harmony with one another; where many forbid exactions, not a few permit them, especially where there is question of a laudable custom, after the administration of the sacrament. When the canons forbid exactions altogether, they do so to consult the welfare of the pastors, because if they mete out canonical penalties to those who defraud them of their rights, many will think they acted from cupidity, rather than from justice and charity. What canons permitted exactions, however, were not new laws, but old and praiseworthy customs; they pertain to superior prelates, who are bound by their office to see to it both that the faithful fulfill their duty towards the pastor, and that the pastors be not deprived of their necessary sustenance.

It was in the thirteenth century that Innocent III [104] gave his official sanction to offerings made by laudable customs, and empowered bishops to force delinquents to abide by them. With this important pronouncement in their favor such offerings were vindicated, and the obligation of observing them was authorized by the common law of the Church.[105]

---

[100] Can. 48 (Mansi, II, 13-14).

[101] Weber, *History of Simony*, Introd., p. 11.

[102] *Capitul. Caroli Magni*, Lib. I, c. 172 (Mansi, XVII^{B}, 857); C. Aix-la-Chapelle, 836, cap. I, can. 5 (Mansi, XIV, 675).

[103] *Vet. et Nov. Eccl. Discipl.*, Pars III, lib. I, cap. LXXII, §7.

[104] IV Lateran C., 1215, can. 66 (Mansi, XXII, 1054).

[105] Cappello, *De Sacramentis*, III, n. 698, 1.

§4. *The Simoniacal Aspect of Stole Fees.*—The practice of giving and receiving the oblations which are now called stole fees is not, and has never been, simoniacal. Church law defines simony of the divine law as: "The deliberate will to buy or sell for a temporal price things intrinsically spiritual, or to buy or sell a temporal thing annexed to a spiritual thing in such a way that the temporal thing cannot exist independently, or to make the spiritual thing even the partial object of a contract." [106]

To establish simony, then, three elements are required: the supernatural object, the temporal price,[107] and the idea of exchange.[108] Ansillon [109] says that the special malice of simony is derived from esteeming spiritual things as of so slight value and temporalities as of so great value that one is traded in compensation for the other. On the contrary, it would seem that the whole malice of simony is seated solely in the third element, the idea of exchange. Theoretically, at least, it would be possible to have the highest appreciation for a spiritual good and to estimate a temporal good as of little value; nevertheless, to exchange one for the other would constitute simony, irrespective of how clearly the inequality between them were recognized. The one thing necessary, therefore, to vindicate the practice of stole fees, and to clear them of all suggestion of simony, is to prove that the idea of exchange for compensation is absent from the practice.

Canon law states equivalently that the custom of proffering stole fees does not fall under the above indictment, declaring that there is no simony when a temporal thing is given, not for a spiritual good, but on the occasion of the latter, and for a just reason recognized by canon law or legitimate custom.[110] It does not, of course, exclude the possibility of simony in particular instances. This must

[106] Can. 727. Transl.: Woywod, *Practical Commentary*, I, n. 613.

[107] "Price" must here be understood in the sense of the Latin *pretium*, a thing of value, so that the idea of transfer may be confined exclusively to the third element.

[108] Weber, *History of Simony*, Introd., p. 3.

[109] *De Simonia in Re Benef.*, cap. XIII, §1.

[110] Can. 730.

be admitted without question, although, incidentally, the Gloss [111] declares that even here it must be externally manifested, otherwise it can neither be proven nor punished. Particular cases, however, in no way militate against a universal custom, and purely mental simony does not enter into the canonical aspect of the subject.[112]

Not content with declaring the practice of stole fees free from simony, the Church has even condemned the proposition that characterizes it as a shameful abuse.[113] Against the corruption of this practice, however, against simony itself, the Church has been equally vehement. From the time that Peter denounced the infamous sin of Simon Magus, down through the centuries the Roman Pontiffs and the Sacred Synods have condemned it,[114] and punished those guilty of it with deposition and excommunication.[115] It is inconceivable, therefore, that the Church could be guilty of such colossal duplicity in reprobating simony and sanctioning a custom that is simoniacal.

It might be argued, however, that Church Law on the subject has been inconsistent, inasmuch as practices that were once forbidden were later sanctioned and approved. For instance, the Council of Elvira,[116] which was the first council to legislate on simony,[117] prohibited even spontaneous oblations at Baptism. Less than three centuries later in the same country (Spain) the Third Council of Braca [118] declared that such spontaneous offerings were acceptable. Again, in the year 494 Pope Gelasius [119] expressly reprobated exactions for Baptism, and this was repeated in numerous councils during the centuries following. Yet in

---

[111] Ad c. 1, C. I, q. 1, v. "*Quidam.*"

[112] Augustine, *Commentary*, IV, p. 6.

[113] Prop. 54 Synodi Pistorien. damn. (Denzinger-Bannwart, *Enchiridion*, No. 1554).

[114] Gibalini, *De Simonia Universa Tract.*, Qu. I, proem.

[115] Devoti, *Inst. Canon.*, Lib. II, tit. IX, §X.

[116] 305, can. 48 (Mansi, II, 13-14).

[117] Weber, *History of Simony*, p. 60 (he adds, "as far as we know").

[118] 572, can. 7 (Mansi, IX, 840).

[119] *Epist. ad Episc. per Lucan.*, cap. 5 (Thiel, *Epist. Rom. Pontif.*, Ep. 14 Gelasii, No. 5, p. 364).

the synodal constitutions of Odo, Archbishop of Paris,[120] there is explicit permission to exact the accustomed offering after the administration of Baptism, and councils in the year 1565 [121] sanctioned the invoking of civil magistrates to enforce customary fees.

In meeting this objection Weber writes:

> Some actions are simoniacal in themselves, by their very nature; others become so in consequence of ecclesiastical prohibition. The Church can evidently abrogate laws which she has framed in virtue of her own merely ecclesiastical authority. Historical circumstances, social conditions, and public opinion may change from one period to another. As a result, certain practices which are prohibited at one epoch as involving a danger or an appearance of simony, may become perfectly lawful with the change in time and environment and the consequent modification in legislation.[122]

The Church frequently forbade such oblations during the first eight centuries [123] because her ministers received sufficient income from tithes and other revenues to insure them decent support.[124] At a later date these sources were to a great extent ceded to collegiate institutions and monasteries,[125] and the ministers of the sacraments were compelled to rely more than previously upon voluntary oblations for their sustenance.[126] When, in securing this source of revenue for pastors, the Church made such oblations obligatory on the part of the faithful, there was no injustice committed against the latter, because their persistence in mak-

---

[120] 1197, cap. 3, n. 2 (Mansi, XXII, 677).

[121] C. Camera, Sect. XVI, cap. VII (Mansi, XXXIII, 1416); C. Milan I, c. 62 (Mansi, XXXIVA, 66 ss.).

[122] *History of Simony*, Introd., p. 10.

[123] Weber, *op. cit.*, p. 11.

[124] Ansillon, *De Simonia in Re Benef.*, cap. XV, §1.

[125] Jessopp, *Nineteenth Century*, XLIII, p. 53; Ansillon, *De Simonia in Re Benef.*, cap. XV, §1.

[126] Ayrinhac, *Constitution of the Church*, No. 271; Ansillon, *l. c.*

ing such offerings was sufficient indication that they wished to bind themselves.[127]

Therefore, wherever laudable custom decrees that an offering be made, the same may be received, asked and exacted without the crime of simony.[128] This holds true even in those instances where pastors have sufficient from other sources to provide for their necessities without depending on such oblations.[129] Nor is there question of simony when such oblations are exacted under threat of ecclesiastical penalties; the exaction is not for spiritualities, for that would be simony, but the penalty is threatened for contumacy in refusing to abide by lawful custom or ecclesiastical statute.[130] Finally, it is also to be noted that when what is exacted exceeds the oblation decreed by lawful custom or legitimate taxation, the sin is one against justice and not of simony.[131]

---

[127] Mostazo, *Tract. de Causis Piis*, Lib. V, cap. XII, 14.

[128] Ugolino, *Tract. de Simonia*, Tab. I, cap. IX, n. 7.

[129] Ansillon, *l. c.*

[130] Ugolino, *op. cit.*, Tab. I, cap. IX, n. 1.

[131] Fanfani, *De Jure Parochorum*, Tit. XII, cap. III, n. 340.

CHAPTER II

THE EVOLUTION AND DEVELOPMENT OF STOLE FEES

The pages immediately following will give in chronological order to the Fourth Lateran Council the conciliar decrees which expressly mention offerings in connection with the three most important functions to which they are attached, namely, baptism, funerals and the nuptial blessing. The purpose of this rather detailed study is to demonstrate certain very important facts in the early evolution of stole fees. It will show the change of attitude with which the ecclesiastical authorities regarded these oblations; the change in the nature of the act of making such offerings, from one of spontaneous devotion to one of obligation; and finally, the trend of this legislation as it regulated the minister's acquisition of such offerings. At first he was forbidden to accept them; then he was prohibited from exacting them but was permitted, tacitly at least, to accept them; and finally, he was explicitly allowed to accept them, and moreover, his superior was empowered and charged to vindicate his right to them.

Article I.—The Period before the IV Lateran Council.

§1. *Baptismal Offerings.*—Anciently it was customary to offer honey and milk at baptism [1] to signify the innocence and suavity to be manifested by those baptized.[2] These were not given as a personal offering to the minister, however, but were consumed by the neophytes themselves.[3]

The Council of Elvira in 305 [4] gives the first record of

[1] C. Africa (*circa* 425), cap. 4 (Mansi, IV, 483).

[2] Thomassin, *Eccl. Discipl.*, Pars III, lib. I, cap. XII, §5.

[3] Devoti, *Inst. Canon.*, Lib. II, tit. XVII, §4.

[4] Can. 48 (Mansi, II, 13-14).

personal offerings on the occasion of baptism. It explicitly states that such offerings were customary, and that thenceforth their acceptance was prohibited. The Third Council of Braca in 572 [5] indicates that the previous decree of Elvira had become obsolete. It permitted voluntary offerings to be accepted, but forbade anything to be exacted from those too poor to give, who, it says, were often deterred from presenting their children for baptism on that account.

The practice of exactions was evidently not new at this time, however, for almost a century before, Pope Gelasius wrote to the Bishops of Lucania, protesting against those who made demands for the administration of baptism.[6] In this letter the Pope expressed the fear that many, out of indignation at such exactions or from poverty, were being deprived of the sacrament. Those who refused to abide by this were to forfeit their "honor." [7]

Exactions for baptism were again proscribed by the Council of Emerita [8] in 666, and by the Council of Toledo [9] in 675, but both decrees expressly permitted the acceptance of voluntary offerings.[10] In England, about the year 748, Lord Ecgbright, Archbishop of York, forbade anything to be asked for baptism, but permitted free-will oblations to be accepted.[11] Excommunication or imprisonment were prescribed for those who offended by demanding a price for their ministrations. The decree of Toledo also inflicted the penalty of temporary excommunication on those guilty of this offense.

---

[5] Can. 7 (Mansi, IX, 840).

[6] *Ep. I ad Episc. per Lucan.*, cap. 5 (Thiel, *Epist. Roman. Pontif.*, Epist. Gelasii 14, n. 5, p. 364).

[7] That is, their share in the offerings of the faithful. Vide Lowrie, *The Church and Its Organization*, p. 328, note I: "The reception of the offerings is 'honor' *par excellence*"; and p. 328, footnote 20: "The priestly honor finds its outward expression in the reception of the offerings."

[8] Can. 9 (Mansi, XI, 81).

[9] Can. 8 (Mansi, XI, 142).

[10] Re decree of Toledo: note * * * to Gratian (c. 101, C. I, q. 1) says that certain codes omit the word "*nisi*"; this would forbid also the acceptance of voluntary offerings.

[11] *Excerptiones Ecgberti*, nn. 12 & 40 (Mansi, XII, 414 & 417).

Simony was very prevalent during the reign of Charlemagne.[12] This may perhaps account for the fact that, though many Councils previous to that time had permitted the practice, his Capitularies [13] prohibited the acceptance of an offering for baptism. The Council of Aix-la-Chapelle [14] in the year 836 likewise forbade pastors to accept such offerings.

Thomassin [15] relates a tale that offers some explanation of the constantly reiterated decrees against exactions, and proves that the apprehension of the ecclesiastical authorities was not unwarranted. In the City of Cologne, about the middle of the ninth century, a certain man endeavored to procure baptism for his infant son. He carried the child through the whole city, asking the different priests to baptize it, and because he was poor and had nothing to offer he was refused. Finally, he explained his difficulty to Saint Herbert, Archbishop of the city, and the latter himself baptized the child.

The Council of Treves [16] in 895 asserted that it was customary to make offerings on the occasion of baptism, but forbade the ministers to demand these oblations. Elfric, later Archbishop of Canterbury,[17] also prohibited such exactions in a list of canons he wrote about the year 957.

In the eleventh and twelfth centuries, five different councils [18] reprobated the practice of making pecuniary demands for the administration of baptism. Towards the end of this century, the synodal constitutions of Odo de Solacio, Archbishop of Paris, ordained that the customary offering for baptism might not only be accepted, but even

---

12 Weber, *History of Simony,* p. 211.

13 Lib. V, c. 172 (Mansi, XVIIB, 857).

14 Cap. I, can. 5 (Mansi XIV, 675).

15 *Eccl. Discipl.,* Pars III, lib. I, cap. LXXI, §10.

16 Cap. 22 (Mansi, XVIIIA, 164).

17 Johnson, *English Canons,* 957, 27.

18 Bourges, 1031, c. 12 (Mansi, XIX, 504-505); Reims, 1049, c. 5 (Mansi, XIX, 742); London, 1125, c. 2 (Mansi, XXI, 330); Westminster, 1138, c. 1 (Mansi, XXI, 511); London, 1175, c. 7 (Mansi, XXII, 149).

exacted, after the sacrament had been conferred.[19] What is noteworthy about this enactment, aside from the express permission to make exactions, is that it used the term "laudable custom" in referring to the practice of making such oblations. This was incorporated into canonical terminology, and for centuries afterwards it was almost invariably used to denote the practice of offering stole fees.

In the beginning of the next century, Innocent III in the IV Lateran Council [20] approved the custom of making such offerings. Thenceforth the general law of the Church permitted the acceptance of these oblations, and ordained that those who were unwilling to abide by such customs should be compelled to do so by their Bishops.[21]

§2. *Funeral Offerings.*—Reverence for the bodies of the dead has ever been a mark of Christian piety, and the clergy have always exercised the greatest diligence in performing the services essential to ecclesiastical sepulture. The Church authorities, while permitting the acceptance of spontaneous offerings made by the faithful on these occasions, have endeavored to protect the practice of making such oblations from all suspicion of simony. At the same time, when this practice gradually won recognition as a laudable custom, its observance, though originally arbitrary, became obligatory.[22]

Offerings were made on the occasion of funeral services from the earliest ages of the Church.[23] From time to time it became necessary to forbid exactions for such services, but it was never forbidden to accept what the relatives, friends or heirs of the deceased spontaneously offered.[24] Tertullian [25] says there is no scriptural precept for oblations for the dead, but that they were authorized by tradition, and custom confirmed the practice of making them.

---

[19] 1197, cap. 3, n. 2 (Mansi, XXII, 677).

[20] 1215, c. 66 (Mansi, XXII, 1054).

[21] C. 42, X, *de simonia*, V, 3.

[22] Thomassin, *Eccl. Discipl.*, Pars III, lib. I, cap. LXVII, §1.

[23] Devoti, *Inst. Canon.*, Lib. II, tit. IX, §VII; Bonal, *Inst. Canon.*, n. 227.

[24] Coronata, *De Locis et Temporibus Sacris*, n. 243.

[25] *De Coron.*, cap. 3 (*MPL*, II, 78-80).

Saint Jerome [26] and Gregory the Great [27] both make mention of offerings for the burying place, but say nothing of offerings for the sacerdotal services.

The Fourth Council of Carthage [28] declared those excommunicate who denied the oblations of the dead to the Church, or who made it difficult to acquire them. Conciliar decrees are silent as regards funeral offerings from that time till the middle of the ninth century, when the Council of Meaux [29] reprobated pecuniary requests but permitted the acceptance of spontaneous oblations; in the year 997 the Council of Ravenna [30] passed a decree to the same effect. At Eanham, in England, it was decreed in the year 1009 that the soul-scot, or funeral offering, should be paid at the open grave,[31] and this injunction was later incorporated into King Cnute's ecclesiastical laws.[32] In 1049 funeral exactions were again proscribed by the Council of Reims.[33]

During the twelfth century five councils [34] reprobated the practice of making demands for sacerdotal services at funerals; two of them, however, expressly stated that it was permissible to accept spontaneous offerings. The decree against exactions was reaffirmed in the year 1200 at Westminster.[35]

In the Fourth Lateran Council,[36] Innocent III approved the practice of making offerings on the occasion of funeral services, and declared that custom had made them oblig-

---

[26] *Liber Quaest. Hebr. in Gen.*, cap. XXIII, v. 16 (*MPL*, XXIII, 272-273).

[27] *Epistolae*, Lib. VIII, ep. 3 ad Episc. Messan. (*MPL*, LXXVII, 907-908).

[28] 398, c. 95 (Mansi, III, 958).

[29] 845, c. 72 (Mansi, XIV, 836).

[30] C. 3 (Mansi, XIX, 220-221).

[31] C. 13 (Mansi, XIX, 307).

[32] 1032, c. 13 (Mansi, XIX, 558).

[33] Can. 5 (Mansi, XIX, 742).

[34] London, 1125, c. 2 (Mansi, XXI, 330); Bourges, 1031, c. 12 (Mansi, XIX, 504-505); Westminster, 1138, c. 1 (Mansi, XXI, 511); London, 1175, c. 7 (Mansi XXII, 149); III Lateran, 1179, c. 7 (Mansi, XXII, 221-222).

[35] Can. 8 (Mansi, XXII, 717-718).

[36] 1215, c. 66 (Mansi, XXII, 1054).

atory for the future. In the Third Lateran Council [37] and again in the year 1198,[38] Innocent III had reprobated exactions made on such occasions, but in the Fourth Lateran decree he stated expressly that the Bishops were to compel those who were unwilling to observe the practice to do so.

§3. *Nuptial Offerings.*—The Council of Trent [39] was the first council to prescribe the pastor's presence for the validity of marriage; before that time a lack of this element did not invalidate the matrimonial contract.[40] From the earliest days of the Church, however, it was customary for the faithful to ask the sacerdotal blessing on their nuptials.[41]

Tertullian was probably the first ecclesiastical writer to record an instance of an offering made on the occasion of the solemnization of matrimony.[42] Blunt thinks that the marriage fee may have had its origin in the appropriation of the gold and silver which were used symbolically in the ancient marriage ceremony.[43]

The first council to make explicit mention of the nuptial offering was a national council held at Westminster in 1138.[44] It forbade under pain of excommunication that any price be asked for this ministration. The Third Lateran Council [45] also prohibited exactions for this function, and declared that long-established customs of making such de-

---

[37] 1179, c. 7 (Mansi, XXII, 221-222).

[38] Resp. *Abbati de Jugo Dei et Priori de Silla,* 28 May, 1198 (C. 39, X, *de simonia,* V, 3).

[39] Sess. XXIV, *de ref. matr.,* cap. 1 (Mansi, XXXIII, 152, 153).

[40] Giraldi, Animadvers. in Barbosa, *De Offic. et Pot. Paroch.,* Pars II, cap. XXI, n. 28.

[41] Westermarck, *History of Human Marriage,* p. 427. Cf. Ignatius, *Epist. ad Polycarp.,* Cap. V (*MPG,* V, 723); C. Carthage IV, 398, c. 13 (Mansi, III, 952, C).

[42] *Ad Uxor.,* lib. II, cap. IX (*MPL,* I, 1302-1303): "Unde sufficiamus ad ennarandam felicitatem ejus matrimonii, quod Ecclesia conciliat, et confirmat oblatio, . . .".

[43] *Book of Church Law,* Bk. II, ch. V, §6: "The ancient Latin rubric is: 'Deinde ponat vir aurum, argentum, et anulum super scutum vel librum'."

[44] Can. 1 (Mansi, XXI, 511).

[45] 1179, c. 7 (Mansi, XXII, 221-222).

mands were insufficient to make them legitimate. It is next mentioned in the year 1198, when Innocent III [46] had occasion to reprimand a chaplain who had made a practice of extorting fees for bestowing the nuptial blessing.

In the Fourth Lateran Council, the custom of making such offerings was expressly approved, but the right to compel the faithful to observe them was reserved to Bishops.[47]

Article II.—The Period Previous to the Code

The councils of the thirteenth century and afterwards, while they make frequent mention of offerings at priestly functions, are for the most part a repetition of the Lateran decree. They refer to it constantly, and very often paraphrase or quote it. Very rarely are the priests forbidden to accept such offerings,[48] but exacting more than the usual amount and extorting offerings before the function are strictly interdicted. Almost invariably they are exhorted to avoid all suspicion of avarice in ministering to the poor. The Bishops are authorized to enforce laudable customs and to punish both those who refuse to abide by them and those guilty of extortion or suspected of simony.

The canonical status of stole fees and of the right to them is now essentially what it was after the Lateran decree.[49] With the exception of offerings made at funerals, which will be treated separately, conciliar decrees and other agents had relatively slight influence on them from that time until the Code. Certain legislation, however, affected the development of some aspects of the subject, and for this reason is worthy of consideration.

§1. *Defining the Amount of Offerings.*—The amount of the offerings for the various functions was determined by

---

[46] Registrum Inn. III, I, 220 (quoted from: c. 39, X, *de simonia,* V, 3).

[47] 1215, c. 66 (Mansi, XXII, 1054).

[48] Saint Charles Borromeo forbade his priests to accept anything, even as an alms, for the administration of the sacraments: Thomassin, *Vet. et Nov. Eccl. Discipl.*, Pars III, lib. I, cap. LXXIII, §4.

[49] Compare canon 463 (C. J. C.) with c. 42, X, *de simonia,* V, 3.

local custom, and although this unwritten law was sufficient to impose an obligation to observe it, the very fact that it was unwritten engendered frequent disputes. It was not until the sixteenth century that the ecclesiastical authorities made definite and intelligent efforts to avoid or lessen such abuses.[50] The remedy was so obvious that it is remarkable it did not suggest itself centuries before, or that the Bishops did not sooner devise this expedient. They had only to define authoritatively the amounts that custom prescribed and half the difficulty would have been solved; if these were consonant with justice and imposed no grave burdens on the faithful, all cause of dissension would have been removed.

The Constitutions of Cardinal Campegius[51] and the Council of Cambrai[52] ordained that Bishops should confer with the civil magistrates of their territories to determine amounts that would be equitable for all.[53] In the Council of Treves[54] the quantity of the offerings for various functions was defined, and it was decreed that nothing more could be demanded. Towards the end of this century the Council of Rouen[55] commanded pastors, with the assistance of their Bishops, if necessary, to consult with their parishioners to determine the amounts of the various offerings.

This practice of determining the fees for different functions is undoubtedly the precedent of canons 1234 and 1507, although in treating this subject the Congregation of the

---

[50] Gasquet (*Parish Life in Med. Eng.*, pp. 131 & 209) and Cutts (*History of English Church*, p. 262) speak of "fixed" fees in England about the thirteenth century. Lesetre (*La Paroisse*, p. 109) states that the amounts for the rural districts differed from those in cities.

[51] 1524, cap. 7 (Mansi, XXXII, 1085, E).

[52] 1565, tit. XVI, cap. VII (Mansi, XXXIII, 1416, B).

[53] Thomassin (*Eccl. Discipl.*, Pars III, lib. I, cap. LXXIII, §2), declares that very early in the sixteenth century Stephen Ponchery, Archbishop of Paris, edited a list of fees for his territory.

[54] 1549, cap. 14 (Mansi, XXXII, 1454, C).

[55] 1581, tit. *de Curat. Offic.*, cap. 26 (Mansi, XXXIV^{A}, 647, B, C, & D).

Council[56] declared that a decree of Innocent XI,[57] issued late in the following century, was the norm to which the latter canon is traceable. That it conclusively demonstrated its utility to the ecclesiastical authorities is evident from the fact that in the eighteenth and nineteenth centuries it was very generally employed.[58]

§2. *Parochial Functions.*—It was sometimes found necessary to insist on the strict observance of parochial jurisdiction, and pastors who offended by administering the sacraments outside their parish limits, or to the parishioners of another pastor, except in grave necessity or with the permission of the proper pastor, incurred penalties of suspension and excommunication.[59] In general, it was well understood that the sacraments were to be received from, and to be administered by, one's proper pastor; he had the exclusive right to assist at Baptism, Marriage and other

---

[56] *Dioecesis M. et Aliarum*, 11 Dec. 1920—*AAS*, XII (1921), 350.

[57] *"Essendosi avuto,"* 8 Oct. 1678 (Cf. text ap. Ferraris, v. *Taxa*, n. 1).

[58] C. Naples, 1699, tit. IX, cap. IV, n. 5 (Mansi, XXXVI^TER^, 778); Avignon, 1725, tit. XXIII, cap. I & tit. XLVII, proem., (Mansi, XXXVII, 311-312 & 362); Synod Mt. Liban., 1736, Appendix, XXXIX, I (Mansi, XXXVIII, 310); Synod Serbor. in Hungaria, 1770-1790, "C" (Mansi, XXXIX, 841-842: a very complete list of twenty-six items with fees indicated); C. Tuam, 1817, Decr. XXVIII (Mansi, XXXIX, 245). The following indicate that the Ordinaries or the diocesan synods were the authorities entitled to define the fees: C. Soissons, 1849, tit. IX, cap. III (Mansi, XLIII, 593); Sens, 1850, tit. IV cap. VII (Mansi, XLIII, 246); Quebec (II), 1854, Decr. XV, §2, No. 8 (Mansi, XLVII, 48-49); Port of Spain (I), 1854, §I, Art. VII, n. 2 (Mansi, XLVII, 66); Ravenna, 1855, Pars III, cap. VI, n. 3 (Mansi, XLVII, 232); Urbino, 1859, Pars I, tit. XV, n. 91 (Mansi, XLVII, 877-878); Quito, 1863, Decr. III, n. 15 (Mansi, XLVIII, 463); Autricourt, 1865 tit. V, cap. VIII (Mansi, XLVIII, 748) & tit. IV, cap. I (Mansi, XLVIII, 702-703); *et al.*

[59] C. London, 1342, cap. XI (Mansi, XXV, 1178, B); Naples, 1699, tit. III, cap. I, n. 2 (Mansi, XXXVI^TER^, 740); Synod. Mt. Liban., 1736, Pars II, cap. I, n. 5 (Mansi, XXXVIII, 41-42); C. Soissons, 1849, tit. IV, cap. II (Mansi, XLIII, 585). See also Ch. I, Art. I, §5, "Laws against Promiscuous Ministration."

functions,[60] especially such as had offerings attached to them by custom or statute. About the right to administer certain functions, however, there were frequent controversies, and in order to put an end to them and the scandal they caused, the Sacred Congregation of Rites, early in the eighteenth century, issued a general decree [61] intended to settle disputed points. Since that time numerous decisions of the Roman Congregations have been based on that decree,[62] but it did not entirely eliminate controversy,[63] and eminent canonists continued to disagree in their definitions of parochial rights, and parochial and sacerdotal functions.[64] Very probably the explanation of this lies in the fact that so many agents can legitimately derogate from common law on this point.[65] In canon 462 the Code enumerates taxatively the functions which are reserved to the pastor by common law, so that there is no longer ground for a difference of opinion on this point, unless there be question of particular customs, indults and so on.

When the Council of Trent [66] made the presence of the pastor an essential for the validity of the matrimonial contract, it was the proper pastor of the parties who was

---

[60] Cf. Reiffenstuel, *Ius Canon. Univers.*, lib. III, tit. XXIX, n. 9; Schmalzgrueber, *Ius Eccl. Univers.*, lib. III, tit. XXIX, n. 9 ss.; *Rituale Romanum*, tit. I, cap. un., *de iis quae in administrand. sacr. generaliter servanda sunt*, n. 17.

[61] "*Urbis et Orbis*," 10 Dec. 1703 (Gardellini, *Decr. Auth. C. S. R.*, No. 3670).

[62] The Congregation of the Council, however, in *Derthonen.*, 7 Dec. 1720 (*Thesaurus*, I, 387), reversed the "response to the sixth doubt" of the decree of 1703, which declared that the blessing of women after childbirth should be performed by their pastors.

[63] Toso, *Ad Cod. J. C. Comment.* (ad can. 462) p. 108, 1.

[64] Wernz-Vidal, *Jus Canonicum*, III, n. 731 (nota (48) ad calc. p. 778).

[65] Most of them are mentioned in the conclusion to the decree of 1703, which reads: "*. . . salvis tamen conventionibus et pactis in erectione confraternitatum forsan factis, concordiis inter partes initis et a Sancta Sede approbatis, indultis, constitutionibus synodalibus, et provincialibus, et consuetudinibus immemorabilibus vel saltem centenariis, . . .*".

[66] 11 Nov. 1563, Sess. XXIV, *de Ref. Matrim.*, cap. I.

meant,[67] so that assistance at this function was reserved to him by common law. The decree *Ne Temere* of August 2, 1907, introduced some changes in the form of marriage, but again the right of the proper pastor of the contracting parties was vindicated, since the liceity of assistance, upon which the right to retain the marriage fee was based, was reserved to him.[68] The difference between this and the preceding legislation on this point is that the proper pastor under the Tridentine decree *Tametsi* was the pastor of domicile or quasi-domicile, while according to the decree *Ne Temere* he was determined either by domicile or by month's residence.[69] These are the antecedents of canon 1097, which revised the law immediately preceding it and restored quasi-domicile as a determinant of the proper pastor for marriage.

§3. *Legislation in the United States.*—In our own country the legislation of the various Baltimore councils during the last century are of some interest, although for the most part they were mere generalizations on the common law of the Church regarding stole fees and parochial rights. The Sixth Provincial Council [70] strictly forbade pastors to baptize or marry those from another diocese whenever it would be convenient for them to receive these sacraments from their proper pastor. The Second Plenary Council [71] prohibited demands for the administration of the sacraments, but permitted the acceptance of voluntary offerings after Baptism and Marriage. It likewise directed Bishops, with the advice of their priests, to establish in their next synod or otherwise a just method of distributing the revenue arising from the administration of Baptism and Matrimony among the clergy residing in the same rectory, having consideration for the greater right and the graver duties

---

67 Cf. *Votum Defensoris Matrim.* ad decr. *Ne Temere—ASS,* XL, 545 & 554 ff.; De Smet, *Betrothment and Marriage,* I, n. 104 (nota (6) ad calc. p. 68).

68 §§V & X—*ASS,* XL, 528, 529.

69 Wernz, *Jus Decretalium,* IV, n. 188.

70 1846, Decr. III (Mansi, XLIII, 7).

71 1866, *Acta et Decreta,* n. 221.

of the pastor.[72] With or without reason, this was disregarded in many dioceses. In the Third Plenary Council [73] the impossibility and inexpediency of having a uniform law on stole fees was recognized and asserted. Each Bishop was admonished to decide this matter for his own territory, either in diocesan synod, or otherwise with the counsel of his diocesan consultors. Whatever taxes they devised were to be submitted to the Holy See for approval.

§4. *Funeral Offerings.*—Besides the offerings which were ordinarily due to the proper pastor of the deceased on the occasion of funerals, custom in some localities sanctioned gifts from the personal property of defunct parishioners. Thus in England during the Middle Ages, the custom of "mortuaries," that is, the gift of the best or second best possession of the deceased, compensated for the fact that the minister's fee was very small.[74] Analogous to this practice was the so-called "Jus Luctuosa" that obtained in Portugal and elsewhere, by which the pastor was entitled to choose for his personal use the best garment, a gold vessel or some other movable possession of the deceased.[75]

The legislation which followed the decree of the Fourth Lateran Council continued to vindicate the pastor's right to funeral offerings,[76] forbidding the soliciting or inducing of laics to elect sepulture away from their proper parishes,[77] and demanding restitution of a part of the funeral offerings whenever parishioners, by reason of ancestral sepulchre or valid election of sepulture, were legitimately buried elsewhere than in their proper parish.[78] The more important and more interesting aspects of it, however, from a canonical as well as from a historical standpoint, were the conciliar decrees and papal bulls which regulated the funeral quarter or parochial portion. For present purposes, there-

---

[72] *Acta et Decreta,* n. 94.

[73] 1884, *Acta et Decreta,* tit. IX, cap. V (p. 168).

[74] Gasquet, *Parish Life in Mediaeval England,* pp. 131 & 132.

[75] Barbosa, *De Offic. et Pot. Paroch.,* Pars III, cap. XXIV, n. 32.

[76] Cf. Thomassin, *Eccl. Discipl.,* Pars III, lib. I, cap. LXVIII.

[77] C. 2, *de treug.,* I, 9 in Extrav. Commun.; c. 1, *de sepult.,* III, 12 in VI°.

[78] C. 1, X, *de sepult.,* III, 28.

fore, it will be sufficient to confine the history of funeral offerings after the Lateran decree to a consideration of the variations in the legal status of the parochial portion; this will of itself prove negatively that funerals and sepulture were strictly parochial functions, and that the proper pastor of the deceased was ordinarily entitled by common law to the offerings made on such occasions.

Article III.—The Parochial Portion

The parochial portion is that part of the funeral offerings to which the pastor is entitled when one of his parishioners is buried outside his proper parish.[79] Formerly it was variously known as the "canonical portion," the "funeral quarter," the "fourth portion," or simply the "justice." [80] Although quantitatively termed the "fourth," it varied in amount according to local custom.[81] In some territories it amounted to one-third or even one-half of the funeral offerings, and these quantities were of obligation wherever sanctioned by legitimate custom;[82] in default of such local determination, however, common law entitled the proper pastor to one-fourth,[83] whence this fraction was frequently employed in the canonical terminology referring to it.

The nature of the parochial portion suggests that it was introduced by law rather than by custom. It is impossible to ascertain definitely when and where this first occurred, although there are certain indications that prove it is of great antiquity. Lingard [84] asserts that in England as early as the year 680 there was a payment legally due to the "shriftshire" or parish of the deceased whenever he was

---

[79] Ojetti, *Synopsis Rerum Moralium et Juris Pontificii*, v. *Quarta Funeraria*, n. 3378; Soglia, *Inst. Jur. Priv. Eccl.*, lib. II, cap. IV, n. 127; Devoti, *Inst. Canon.*, lib. II, tit. IX, §VIII; Mostazo, *Tract. de Causis Piis*, lib. I, cap. XII, n. 41.

[80] Coronata, *De Locis et Temporibus Sacris*, n. 247.

[81] Ojetti, Devoti et Soglia, *ls. cs.*

[82] C. 9, X, *de sepult.*, III, 28.

[83] C. 8, X, *de sepult.*, III, 28.

[84] *History and Antiquities of the Anglo Saxon Church*, I, p. 192.

buried elsewhere. The Council of Eanham [85] and Cnute's Ecclesiastical Laws [86] likewise decreed that this "soul-scot," which was the whole funeral offering, and not merely a part of it,[87] was due under the same circumstances. Although these fees are analogous to the funeral quarter, and may even be local interpretations of it, it is improbable that they represent the antecedent of the canonical parochial portion. Certainly the decrees of Eanham and Cnute cannot be such since they were promulgated two centuries subsequent to the decree *"Nos Instituta"* of Pope Leo III,[88] which refers to the canonical portion as a then long-established institution. There are no existing records antedating the decree of Leo that mention the parochial portion as such, or any practice closely resembling it. This same document asserts the right of the faithful to elect the place of their sepulture, and to be buried in the sepulture of their ancestors if they die not having made such election, and it mentions these as the instances when the parochial portion is due.

Authors are practically unanimous in explaining the pastor's right to this part of the funeral offerings as being based on the administration of the sacraments and the constant care which he exercised over the spiritual welfare of the deceased,[89] and this is confirmed by the regulations for determining the church to which it was to be paid. Where the deceased pertained to but one parish, this was evidently the one which was entitled to the parochial portion. When he belonged to two parishes, if he actually lived in both places and spent part of his time in one and part in the other, the portion was to be divided between these parishes;[90] but if he attended Mass in one parish

---

[85] 1009, tit. *De Censu Lumin. et Sepult.* (Mansi, XIX, 301).

[86] 1032, c. 13 (Mansi, XIX, 558).

[87] Johnson, *English Canons,* 1017, 13, note.

[88] C. 1, X, *de sepult.*, III, 28.

[89] Barbosa, *De Offic. et Pot. Paroch.*, Pars III, cap. XXV, n. 1; *Idem, De Offic. Episc.*, Pars III, alleg. LXXV, n. 46; Soglia, *Inst. Jur. Priv. Eccl.*, lib. II, cap. IV, n. 127; Devoti, *Inst. Canon.*, lib. II, tit. IX, §VIII; Mostazo, *Tract. de Causis Piis,* lib. I, cap. XII, n. 41.

[90] C. 2, *de sepult.*, III, 12 in VI°.

and received the sacraments in another, the parochial portion was due to that parish in which he was accustomed to receive the sacraments.[91]

As with the quantity of the portion, so also regarding the offerings from which it might be demanded, local custom played an important part.[92] Ordinarily it was due from all the offerings made to the pastor and the church for the funeral itself and on the occasion of it, whether these consisted merely of the oblations due by custom or statute, or included others prompted by the generosity of the deceased.[93] It was not, however, to be deducted from what was left for divine cult, or for the exequies of the third, seventh, twentieth and thirtieth days and anniversaries.[94] As an exception to this, the Friars Preachers and the Friars Minor were for a time obliged to return a fourth portion of everything they acquired from those who had elected sepulture with them,[95] but they later acquired new exemptions which derogated from this obligation.[96]

Exemption from the obligation to pay the parochial portion was obtained by custom, prescription and pontifical privilege. The Council of Trent[97] decreed that, notwithstanding privileges to the contrary, all monasteries, hospitals and other pious places, which for forty complete years previous to the Council,[98] had not been free of the obligation to pay the portion, could not be considered exempt, and were therefore subject to the prescripts of common law on this point. A few years later, Pope Pius V, in his constitution *"Etsi Mendicantium,"*[99] declared that all monasteries founded after 1523, which pertained to an Order legitimately exempted from paying the portion, were

[91] Barbosa, *De Offic. et Pot. Paroch.*, Pars II, cap. XXV, n. 24.

[92] Reiffenstuel, *Jus Canon. Univers.*, lib. III, tit. XXVIII, n. 52.

[93] C. 10, X, *de sepult.*, III, 28; Many, *De Locis Sacris*, n. 204, 1° & 3°.

[94] C. 20, X, *de testament.*, III, 26.

[95] C. 2, *de sepult.*, III, 7 in Clem.

[96] Many, *De Locis Sacris*, n. 204, 3° (nota ad calc. p. 328).

[97] Dec. 3, 1563, Sess. XXV, *de Ref.*, cap. 13.

[98] That is, from the year 1523 (Many, *op. cit.*, n. 203, 1°, a).

[99] 16 May 1567, §2, n. 11 (Bull. Rom., VII, 579).

likewise to be considered exempt in this respect. Since this was an interpretation of the Tridentine decree it was not affected by the subsequent bull of Gregory XIII,[100] which reduced other concessions of the previous document to the limits of common law. In 1605, Paul V [101] confirmed an interpretation of the decision of the Council of Trent in favor of the Order of Carmelites. Finally, Benedict XIII, in his constitution "*Romanus Pontifex*," [102] abolished all privileges of not paying the portion in Italy and its adjacent islands, so that thereafter in this territory there was no claim to exemption on the basis of privilege.

Besides those mentioned above, there were other privileges of exemption conceded after the Council of Trent, and any which were not revoked by the decree of Benedict XIII, still obtain. In many places, however, custom has entirely abolished the practice, and the obligation as well, of paying the parochial portion.[103]

The Code of Canon Law introduced some modifications of the legislation that preceded it. For example, it eliminated the necessity of determining where the deceased fulfilled his religious duties by basing the right to the portion on the simple fact of parochial domicile or quasi-domicile. Again, common law formerly demanded that the portion be paid, irrespective of the distance from the place of death to the proper parish;[104] as an exception to this, canon 1236, §1, declares that this obligation does not exist when transfer of the corpse to its proper parish is inconvenient. Finally, the new law limits the sources from which the portion is deducted to what is stated for funeral and burial in the schedule of diocesan fees.

---

[100] "*In tanta*," 1 Mar. 1573, §6 (Bull. Rom., VIII, 40).

[101] Const. "*Decet Romanum*," 20 Aug. 1605, §3 (Bull. Rom., XI, 216).

[102] 28 Apr. 1725, §§3 & 4 (Bull. Rom., XXII, 149-150).

[103] *Cath. Encycl.*, VI, v. "*Funeral Dues.*"

[104] Many, *De Locis Sacris*, n. 202, 4°; Rossi, *Sepult. Eccl. e l' Ius Funer.*, n. 98 (nota ad calc. p. 185); Coronata, *De Loc. et Temp. Sacr.*, n. 248, f).

PART II

Canonical Aspect

CHAPTER III

General Law on Stole Fees

Article I.—The Acquisition of Stole Fees

Canon 463.—§1. Ius est parocho ad praestationes quas ei tribuit vel probata consuetudo vel legitima taxatio ad normam can. 1507, §1.

§2. Potiores exigens, ad restitutionem tenetur.

§3. Licet paroeciale aliquod officium ab alio fuerit expletum, praestationes tamen parocho cedunt, nisi de contraria offerentium voluntate certo constet circa summam quae taxam excedit.

§4. Gratuitum ministerium ne deneget parochus iis qui solvendo pares non sunt.

With an argument based on an investigation into the legal signification of the word *"praestatio,"* [1] Augustine [2] contends that by this word "the law intends to comprise the whole range of income, salary and stole-fees, with the sole exception of manual mass stipends." Whatever may be said of its bearing on other revenues, it is certain from the text of the canon and from its reference to canon 1507, §1, that it pertains directly and immediately to stole fees, and that all regulations governing such offerings must be in conformity with the prescripts given here. Since salaries and other ecclesiastical incomes do not come within the scope of this treatise, canon 463 will be considered here only in so far as it applies to stole fees.

[1] Cf. Dig. 43, 26; Du Cange, *Glossarium*, v. *"Praestatio"*; can. 1410.
[2] *Commentary*, II, 541.

§1. *The Functions of Custom.*—In speaking of oblations, it is almost impossible to overestimate the importance of custom; from beginning to end this subject resolves itself into a question of legitimate custom.[3] That this is true of stole fees is immediately apparent from canon 463, §1, as well as from what was said of custom in a previous chapter.[4] A strictly literal interpretation of this passage —which, from the carefully indefinite wording of it, is obviously the interpretation which the legislator intends it to receive—makes three points evident, namely, that custom (or legitimate taxation, of which more below) determines whether or not the pastor is entitled to receive such fees; that the functions to which stole fees are attached are indicated by custom; and, finally, that the amount of the offerings is determined by the same source.

To say that stole fees can be ceded otherwise than to the pastor may at first glance seem contrary to the wording of the law. The history of these offerings also would seem to indicate that such a practice is unlawful; they were given to the pastor, for his sustenance where other revenues were lacking or insufficient for this purpose, to use as he pleased where his ordinary needs were supplied from other sources. Moreover, it is apparently opposed to the tenor of Church Law, which has always considered as sacred the intention of the donor regarding the destination and administration of pious offerings. In consideration of the foregoing, therefore, there would seem to be little justification for a statute which, for example, directs that the revenue arising from stole fees be applied to defray the current expenses of the rectory with its clerical and lay personnel.

Against this view of the question, however, there is the fact that, if the pastor is assigned nothing by approved custom or legitimate taxation, or if he is given only the administration of stole fees, there is no violence done to the literal sense of canon 463, §1. Moreover, this is only

---

[3] Ferraris, v. *Oblationes*, n. 31; Barbosa, *De Offic. et Pot. Paroch.*, Pars III, cap. 24, n. 31; S. C. C., *Lucana*, 17 Dec. 1904—*ASS*, XXXVII, 700.

[4] Ch. I, art. II, §§2 & 3.

apparently contrary to the spirit of this law, for the legislator's intention on this particular point, as far as this can be deduced from the wording of the law, was evidently twofold: first, to permit custom and diocesan statute, which have always been the determining factors in any question of stole fees, to continue to exert their influence; and secondly, to guarantee and protect by common law the pastor's right to stole fees in those territories where they are assigned to him. Another argument to support this view is derived from the fact that customs substantially identical with the example given in the preceding paragraph have obtained for a considerable time in various places; they are authorized by provincial councils containing, or permitting Bishops to make, statutes to that effect. That they are legitimate is obvious, first because they have not been repudiated by any Roman Congregation, and secondly, because they require the approval of the Holy See [5] before they obtain the force of law. As to the objection based on the intention of the donor, that is sufficiently met by the assertion of Pope Leo XIII [6] that the will of private individuals, even regarding pious offerings, cannot be permitted to defeat the purpose of a law intended to promote the common good. Apropos of the preceding argument, this same constitution [7] sanctioned the decree of the Second

[5] Can. 291, §1.

[6] Const. "*Romanos Pontifices,*" 8 May 1881, §26—*Fontes*, No. 582 (III, 184): ". . . Praeterea si in parochum rectoremve, a quibus spiritualia adiumenta fideles accipiunt, haud inconcinne praesumi potest collata liberalitas, ubi Ecclesia bonis praedita sit, per quae religionis decori et ministrorum tuitioni prospiciatur, longe aliud iudicium esse debet ubi eam bonorum copiam Ecclesia non habeat, ac liberalitate fidelis populi unice aut potissimum sustentetur. Tunc enim largitores putandi forent voluisse consulere cultus divini splendori et religionis dignitati, ea ratione et modo quem ecclesiastica auctoritas decerneret . . . . Legis porro sese interponens auctoritas, si largitionum tempora et causas praestituat, illud efficit quoque, ne fideles semper pro arbitrio possint modum et finem designare in quem oblatam stipem erogari oporteat; nequit enim facere privatorum voluntas, ut quod a legitima potestate in bonum commune praecipitur certo destituatur effectu. . . ."

[7] *Ibidem.*

Provincial Council of Westminster to the effect that stole fees "should ordinarily be considered as belonging to the priests; though they are distributed in different ways, in different places. That distribution seems to be the best, which is most conducive to alleviate the burthen of the mission . . . we leave it to the prudence of Bishops to determine in their diocesan synods what seems best adapted to the customs and state of places. . . ." [8]

Where household expenses come from stole fees it might happen in very rare instances that there would be a surplus. In this event it would be unjustifiable to apply this surplus to the church, the poor or any other purpose; it should be divided equally among the clergy of the parish,[9] since these have an equal right to what they all would have enjoyed had they lived on a more lavish scale. Nor can the pastor, if he has assistants, vindicate this surplus to himself for the same reason. To admit the contrary would lead in some instances to the practice of economies that would inflict hardship and privation on the assistants.

That custom determines the functions to which stole fees are attached is equally evident from this canon. These functions are called parochial functions in contradistinction to those which are merely sacerdotal; the right to assist at the former is reserved to the pastor, while the latter may be performed by any priest.[10] Offerings made at these functions are distinguished in the same way: those made at parochial functions are strictly parochial offerings and belong to the pastor; those made at merely sacerdotal functions belong to the priest who assists at the function.[11] Strictly parochial functions are taxatively [12] enumerated in canon 462; that is to say, these, and these only, are reserved

---

[8] 1855, nn. 15 & 16 (Mansi, XLVII, 275-276); transl. by Guy, *The Synods in English*, p. 162. Cf. C. Plen. Balt. II, 1866, *Acta et Decreta*, n. 94; S. C. C., in *Parisien.*, 9 Sept. 1848 (Lingen et Reuss, "*Causae Selectae*," n. 475).

[9] Smith, *Notes on the Second Plenary Council of Baltimore*, p. 84.

[10] Cocchi, *Comment. in Cod. I. C.*, lib. II, n. 341; De Meester, *Juris Canonici Compendium*, II, n. 822, 1°.

[11] S. C. C., in *Lucana*, 17 Dec. 1904—*ASS*, XXXVII, 701.

[12] *Ius Pontificium*, VIII (1928), 155.

to the pastor by common law. Local custom, however, can make other functions, not enumerated in this canon, strictly parochial. The blessing of women after childbirth suggests itself as a notable example. By common law this is not reserved to the pastor, yet in certain territories, Belgium, for example,[13] it has become such through local custom.

Nowhere in the Code is it stated that parochial functions must have an offering, or stole fee, attached to them. Canon 1234 gives certain regulations to govern funeral offerings, and canon 1097, §3, presupposes that offerings are made on the occasion of weddings, but with these exceptions there is no direct mention of stole fees in connection with parochial functions. The silence of the legislator on this point is an obvious indication that it is left to local custom to determine what functions shall have stole fees attached to them, and canonists who comment on this question are agreed that this is the case.[14]

The third function of custom, in the absence of diocesan statutes on the subject, is to determine the amount of the stole fees for each function. Pastors have no authority to depart from this norm,[15] and when they demand more than custom or statute decrees they are bound to restitution.[16] The obligation here is one of justice; what must be repaid, however, is not the whole offering, but only that part of it which is in excess of the amount to which they are entitled. It is to be noted, moreover, that the delinquent in this instance does not incur the penalties decreed against simony,[17] since the offering is not given in payment for a spirituality, but merely on the occasion of a spiritual ministration and for a reason admitted by canon law.[18] He does, however, render himself liable to the penalties of canon 2408, which prescribes that a heavy fine be imposed on those guilty of

---

13 *Collationes Brugenses*, XXIII (1923), 79.

14 Ojetti, *Synopsis*, *v. Jura Stolae*, n. 2554; Vogt, *Das kirchliche Vermögensrecht*, §39, 2.

15 Pallotini, *Collectio Resolutionum S. C. C.*, XIV, v. *Parochus*, §VII, n. 19; Berardi, *De Parocho*, n. 927; Vogt, *l. c.*

16 Can. 463, §2.

17 Fanfani, *De Jure Parochorum*, n. 240.

18 Can. 730.

this crime; one who offends repeatedly is to be suspended or removed from office according to the gravity of his guilt, and these penalties in no way release him from the obligation of repaying what he has unjustly acquired.

Voluntary offerings in excess of the customary fee are wholly acceptable, and the recipient in retaining them does not incur the penalties just mentioned. However, they must result from the generosity of the faithful; the minister is not permitted either directly or indirectly to ask for more than the customary fee.[19]

§2. *Legitimate Taxation.*—What has been said of custom is substantially true of legitimate taxation. Canon 463, §1, indicates that this taxation must be in accordance with the prescripts of canon 1507, §1, which states that it is the office of a provincial council or of a convention of the bishops of the province, to determine the fees that are to be paid throughout the whole province on the occasion of the administration of sacraments and sacramentals.[20] The principle on which this canon is based is contained in canon 1496, where it is affirmed that the Church has the right, independent of the civil authority, to demand of the faithful whatever is necessary for divine worship, the sustenance of the clergy and other ministers, and for other purposes peculiar to her.

Almost invariably it will be found that statutes which enumerate such fees are merely the mutation into actual laws of customs that have already possessed the binding force of laws. By the unanimous consent of doctors, only one reason other than legitimate custom is admitted as sufficient to justify making such offerings obligatory, namely, the necessity of providing for the clergy when they would otherwise lack means of sustenance.[21]

Innocent XI [22] devised the norm upon which the subject

---

[19] Can. 736.

[20] Funeral fees are regulated by canon 1234, which will be treated later.

[21] Bouix, *De Parocho*, Pars IV, cap. IX, §1, qu. 5a, 1°.

[22] "*Essendosi avuto,*" 8 Oct. 1678 (cf. text. ap. Ferraris, v. *Taxa*, n. 1.

matter of canon 1507 is modeled.[23] That part of it which refers to fees on the occasion of the administration of the sacraments, however, is directly traceable to a general decree of the Congregation of the Council issued on the 10th of June, 1896.[24] This document explicitly denied the legality of leaving the specific determination of fees in the various dioceses to the judgment of the local Ordinaries.[25] That canon 1507, §1 confirms this is declared in the decision of 1920, which explains that the wording of this canon makes it evident that local Ordinaries have no power to determine these fees, since the one case where they have such authority [26] is explicitly excepted. The schedule of fees, therefore, must be determined by the provincial council or by the convention of the Bishops of the province. They may not devise a scale or list the maximum and minimum fees acceptable, leaving it to the Ordinaries to determine more specifically what fees must be observed in their respective dioceses.[27] This is evident from the purpose of the law which, as stated in the two decrees of the Congregation of the Council which preceded it, is to secure and preserve

---

[23] S. C. C., *Dioecesis M. et Aliarum,* 11 Dec. 1920—*AAS,* XIII (1921), 350.

[24] *Normae quoad taxas—ASS,* XXIX, 433-435.

[25] Ad II. A former decree, S. C. C. in *Parisien,* 9 Sept. 1848 (Lingen et Reuss, "*Causae Selectae,*" n. 475), admitted the Bishop's authority in this matter: ". . . Observandum insuper est ad Episcopum pertinere praefatorum emolumentorum taxätiones in synodo vel extra edere. . . ." Despite the decision of 1896 and the prescripts of the Code, it is probable that in particular instances 'for a legitimate cause and when the utility of the diocese demands it,' the Bishop can regulate matters pertaining to stole fees and parochial functions in a manner that may be contrary to general law. Cf. Benedict XIV, *Inst. Eccl.,* 105, nn. 94 & 95; S. R. Rota, in *Theatina,* 23 Mar. 1911—*AAS,* III (1911), 424-425; Berardi, *De Parocho,* n. 927; Mater, *L'Eglise Catholique,* p. 427.

[26] Can. 1234, where they are authorized to determine funeral fees with the advice of the cathedral chapter or their diocesan consultors.

[27] S. C. C., *Dioecesis M. et Aliarum,* 11 Dec. 1920—*AAS,* XIII (1921), 351. A question of chancery taxes gave rise to this decision, but from the decree itself it is clear that it applies also to the determination of fees on the occasion of administering sacraments and sacramentals.

uniformity in the whole province, and to avoid the contentions and scandal which might otherwise result. Moreover, even though it be published prematurely, this schedule has no juridical effect until it has been approved by the Congregation of the Council.[28]

Canons 736 and 2408 apply to legitimate taxation as well as to the fees sanctioned by custom. The latter, as was stated above, enumerates the penalties against those who demand more than the determined fee; the former makes the list of functions for which fees may be asked practically taxative, so that they may not be demanded on other occasions unless justified by legitimate custom.

§3. *The Recipient of Stole Fees.*—By "pastor" here—and elsewhere in these pages unless otherwise specified—is meant the priest in whom the title to a parish is vested and who actually exercises the office of pastor, that is, the physical person who is at one and the same time both actual and habitual pastor. To state that a physical person can be the habitual pastor of a parish is contrary to the views of many modern canonists, who *define* the habitual pastor as a moral person,[29] and who assert that habitual pastors cannot exercise the care of souls.[30] It is difficult to see how these assertions are justified by the canons (452, §2, and 471, §1) on which they are based; these canons actually presuppose the divisibility of the pastoral office into actual and habitual elements, and prescribe that when a moral person holds title to the office of pastor it can retain only the habitual element, the habitual care of souls, and that the actual care of souls must be assigned to a physical person, the vicar curator. That their conclusions are not substantiated by pre-Code law is evidenced by Barbosa,[31] who speaks casually of one subject invested with both ac-

[28] Cans. 250, §2, 291, §1 & 1507, §1; S. C. Consist., 21 Apr. 1910—*AAS*, II (1910), 329-330.

[29] Fanfani, *De Jure Parochorum*, n. 85; Vermeersch-Creusen, *Epitome*, I, n. 493, 1.

[30] Wernz-Vidal, *Ius Canonicum*, II, n. 720, a); Cocchi, *Comment. in Cod. I. C.*, lib. II, n. 333.

[31] *De Offic. et Pot. Paroch.*, Pars I, cap. I, nn. 64 & 77; S. C. C., in *Melevitana*, 27 Aug. 1904—*ASS*, XXXVII, 104.

tual and habitual care of souls. Moreover, it would seem impossible to reconcile their views with the prescripts of canons 452, §1, and 1423, §2. If, as these canons seem to imply, the elements of both actual and habitual pastor are not already inherent in the office of pastor, how then can they be divided, as happens when, in the union of a parish to a moral person, the title to the office of habitual pastor is conferred on the moral person, while the actual care of souls is left to the pastor or vicar?

It is not from any arbitrary motive or from a spirit of controversy that the above exception is made. If it can be validly premised that the actual and habitual care of souls can exist simultaneously in one individual, then the way is paved for the statement of a principle or axiom by which the rights of the various pastors and vicars to stole fees can be measured and defined. That principle, in so far as it is apparent from the practice of the Roman Curia and from the works of authoritative canonists, is that stole fees, according to the common law of the Church, belong to the habitual pastor of the parish. The influence of custom, diocesan statutes, episcopal decrees and other agents upon this right of habitual pastors can best be explained by a brief reference to the various priests who can exercise the actual care of souls.

Whenever the actual and the habitual care are united in one physical person, as in the pastor and the quasi-pastor, there is no question of another's right to stole fees without derogation to common law.[32] The same holds true for the vicar oeconomus, who is appointed by the Ordinary to fulfill the duties of pastor or quasi-pastor when either of these offices becomes vacant.[33] Since, temporarily at least, he exercises both habitual and actual care of the parish, he is entitled to receive the stole fees[34] until a new incumbent is appointed to the vacant office. If, however, in accordance with canon 1410, stole fees are considered as part of

---

[32] That is, through custom or particular law; the wording of canon 463, §1 admits the liceity of this.

[33] Cans. 472, §1 & 473, §1.

[34] Wernz-Vidal, *Ius Canonicum,* II, n. 741, III; De Meester, *Juris Canonici Compendium,* II, n. 869, III, a).

the fruits of the benefice, it would seem to be within the jurisdiction of the local Ordinary to decide whether or not the vicar oeconomus can claim them in addition to whatever other remuneration is assigned to him.[35]

When a moral person is the habitual pastor of a parish, the provisions of canons 452, §2, and 471, §1, demand that the actual care of souls be confided to a vicar curator. In this case, according to the principle given above, the habitual pastor receives the stole fees.[36] However, either the Bishop, in determining the remuneration of the vicar curator by authority of canon 471, §1, or the articles regulating the economy of the parish, may assign to him the right to participate in the stole fees.[37]

A vicar substitute fulfills the office of pastor either when the latter is absent or when he has been deprived of his parish but suspends the execution of the sentence by recourse to higher authority.[38] In the former hypothesis the stole fees belong to the absent pastor, who, since it is a question of alienating what is strictly his own property, is at liberty to include them or not in the remuneration he offers his substitute; in the second case, if the Ordinary does not concede them to the substitute, they are to be reserved until the pastor's claims are sustained or denied.[39]

When, on account of the physical, mental or moral incapacity of the pastor, a vicar adjutor is appointed to fulfill, either wholly or in part, the office of pastor, the latter is still entitled to receive the stole fees, unless the local Ordinary in determining the recompense of the vicar adjutor assigns them to him.[40]

---

[35] Can. 472, §1.

[36] Cf. De Luca, *De Parochis*, Disc. XXII, n. 7; S. C. C., in *Melevitana*, 27 Aug. 1904—*ASS*, XXXVII, 104-105.

[37] Bened. XIV, Const. *"Cum semper oblatas,"* 19 Aug. 1744 (*Fontes*, I, n. 345); Giraldi, animadvers. ad Barbosa (*De Offic. et Pot. Paroch.*), Pars I, cap. II, n. 154; De Luca, *De Parochis*, Disc. XVIII, n. 12; S. C. C., in *Melevitana*, 20 Dec. 1902—*ASS*, XXXV, 346-349.

[38] Can. 474.

[39] Wernz-Vidal, *Ius Canonicum*, II, n. 742, III.

[40] Wernz-Vidal, *Ius Canonicum*, II, n. 742, III; Ayrinhac, *Constitution of the Church*, n. 299.

The right of a vicar cooperator, that is, of a curate or assistant pastor, to participate in stole fees depends upon custom, diocesan statute, episcopal decree or the will of the pastor.[41] While common law assigns them no part in these oblations,[42] the custom of sharing stole fees with the assistants, which was recommended to our Bishops by the Second Plenary Council of Baltimore,[43] is now almost universally observed.[44]

Military and naval chaplains must determine their rights to stole fees from their letters of deputation; if these omit all mention of the subject, the principle may be followed that, whenever they assist licitly at a function to which a stole fee is attached, they are entitled to retain the same. The rights of other chaplains to retain stole fees will be considered in the chapter on Exemption.

§4. *The Relation between the Donor and the Recipient.*—Parochiality is the relation that must ordinarily exist between the pastor and the donor of stole fees in order that the former may licitly retain such offerings. His right to administer the sacraments and sacramentals which are considered parochial functions—and consequently to receive the fees attached to them—is territorial, personal and exclusive.[45] Outside the limits of his parish, therefore, he has ordinarily no authority to act at these functions, even in behalf of his own parishioners; within his parish limits the same holds true regarding those of another parish, unless in particular cases necessity or some other legitimate cause permits him to act.[46]

Corresponding to and arising from this right of pastors,

---

[41] Can. 476, §6; Wernz-Vidal, *op. cit.*, II, n. 744, III; Bargilliat, *Droits et Devoirs des Cures et des Vicaires Paroissiaux*, n. 547, b); Ayrinhac, *op. cit.*, n. 305; Cocchi, *Comment. in. Cod. I. C.*, lib. II, n. 370, b).

[42] S. C. C., in *Lucana*, 17 Dec. 1904—*ASS*, XXXVII, 701; Pallotini, *Collectio Resolutionum S. C. C.*, XIV, v. *Parochus*, §VII, n. 16.

[43] *Acta et Decreta*, n. 94.

[44] Cocchi, *l. c.* This cannot be asserted of the United States.

[45] Wernz-Vidal, *Ius Canonicum*, II, n. 731.

[46] This prescinds from the fact that he acts licitly whenever he has the permission of the pastor either of the parish or of the parties in question.

there is an obligation on the part of the faithful to present themselves and their charges to their proper pastor on these occasions. The reason for this has already been explained;[47] the gravity of the obligation may be gauged from the fact that Laymann [48] and others consider parents guilty of grave sin who present their child other than to their proper pastor for baptism without the latter's permission.

The faithful determine their proper pastor either by domicile or by quasi-domicile; the former is acquired by actual residence for a period of ten years or by taking up residence with the intention of remaining always; the latter, either by actual residence for the greater part of a year, or by taking up residence with the intention of remaining for at least the greater part of a year.[49] To all practical purposes the effects of domicile and of quasi-domicile, except as regards the sacrament of Holy Orders, to which this treatise has no reference, are identical.[50] These effects can be better understood by considering them separately in their relation to the individual functions. For the present, therefore, it will be sufficient to cite a few general principles that apply everywhere. These are: first, that children under twenty-one retain the domicile of their parents or guardians, but can acquire their own quasi-domicile when they have reached the age of seven;[51] second, that wives have the same domicile as their husbands but can acquire their own quasi-domicile and, if legitimately separated, their own domicile;[52] third, that the proper pastor of those who have no parochial domicile or quasi-domicile is the pastor of the place where they are actually staying.[53]

Finally, it is to be noted by way of exception that in

---

[47] See Ch. I, Art. I, §5.

[48] *Theol. Moral.*, lib. V, tr. 2, cap. 7, n. 2; Barbosa, *De Offic. et Pot. Paroch.*, Pars II, cap. XVIII, n. 1.

[49] Cans. 94, §1 and 92, §§1 & 2.

[50] Vindex, "Domicilium et Quasi-Domicilium," *Ius Pontificium*, VI (1926), 158.

[51] Can. 93, §§1 & 2.

[52] *Ibidem.*

[53] Can. 94, §§2 & 3.

some localities the payment of pew rent is considered equivalent to the acquisition of domicile in so far as it entitles the pastor to administer all sacraments, even those considered parochial functions, to all who pay pew rent, though territorially some of these may not be his parishioners.[54]

§5. *The Title to Stole Fees.*—Canon 463, §1, declares that the pastor has a *right* to stole fees. According to the principles of all law a right permits one to demand that to which one is entitled. The pastor, then, is authorized by this canon to demand of the faithful whatever custom or taxation assigns to him. Since "right" and "obligation" are correlative terms, it follows necessarily that the faithful are bound to respect this right. The pastors themselves, however, have no authority to enforce this obligation;[55] moreover, they are not permitted to refuse their services when the offering is not forthcoming—and prudence, decency and respect for holy things dictate that ordinarily there should be no mention of money before an ecclesiastical function. Nevertheless, it would be futile to secure this right to pastors if there were no means to safeguard it and to enforce the unwilling to abide by the obligation it induces. In conformity with the decree of the Fourth Lateran Council [56] and the traditional and consistent interpretation of that law,[57] the Code does this in canon 2349,

[54] "The payment of pew rent in another church does not of itself confirm membership in that parish, nor grant to that pastor the right to exercise parochial functions. There exists, however, in many dioceses an old custom, sometimes reënforced by synodal regulations, which permits the pastor of the Church in which the pew is held to administer all the sacraments to his pew-holders wherever they reside. If such a custom or regulation does not exist, the pastor of the parish of actual residence must be summoned." *Amer. Eccl. Rev.*, LXXIV (1926), 413. Cf. Synodus Dioecesana Syracusensis XI (1921), n. 64. The reasonableness of this custom is undoubtedly open to question.

[55] Reiffenstuel, *Jus Canon. Univers.*, lib. V, tit. III, n. 192; Laymann, *Theol. Moral.*, lib. IV, tr. X, cap. VIII, §II, n. 16.

[56] 1215, c. 66 (Mansi, XXII, 1054); c. 42, X, *de simonia*, V, 3.

[57] Reiffenstuel, *Jus Canon. Univers.*, lib. IV, tit. III, n. 192 & lib. III, tit. XXVIII, n. 71; Laymann, *Theol. Moral.*, lib. IV, tr. X, cap. VIII, §II, n. 16; Devoti, *Inst. Canon.*, lib. II, tit. XVII, n. 6; Soglia, *Inst. Jur. Priv. Eccl.*, lib. II, cap. IV, n. 73; Smith, *Counterpoints in Canon Law*, nn. 196, 197.

where the Ordinary is empowered to compel recusants to satisfy this obligation with whatever punishments his prudent judgment dictates.

It follows from the nature of this right that it is not within the jurisdiction of pastors to renounce it, even though they have sufficient revenue from other sources to care for their necessities. It is not a personal privilege and it is not conceded to pastors individually; rather, it is founded on common law and is conceded to pastors as such. Under these circumstances to renounce this right would be to prejudice the rights, not only of their successors, but of pastors in common, which they are evidently bound to preserve. When, therefore, the faithful committed to their care either frequently or flagrantly refuse to make the offerings which custom or statute prescribes, pastors are bound to bring this fact to the attention of the Ordinary. The reasons for this are evident: the Ordinary is bound by his office to safeguard these rights, and he has no other means of acquiring this knowledge. Moreover, pastors can as effectually prejudice the right to these offerings by their negligence as by any positive act contrary to it. It is probable, however, that if violations of this right are rare and not likely to give scandal or to lead others to disregard it, there is no necessity to bring them to the notice of the proper authorities, first, because the harm they do is relatively slight, and secondly, because there is equivalent danger of giving scandal if a pastor appears unreasonably jealous of his right.

It does not follow from this, however, that customs and statutes regarding stole fees are immutable. Regarding the amount of the offering, it is certain that if custom can determine this it can also change it,[58] and the same is evidently true of legitimate taxation. Moreover, since under the proper circumstances customs and laws can be abrogated by contrary customs and laws,[59] it is not impossible for stole fees legitimately to be abolished in a given terri-

---

[56] Cappello, *De Visitat. SS. Limin.*, Vol. II, cap. VII, tit. 70, sect. VII, n. 5.

[59] Cans. 22, 27 and 30.

tory. Cappello[60] states that the only condition requisite for this is that the pastors have sufficient revenues from other sources to support themselves. That they may be abolished with the consent of the proper authorities is also true; there is record of such a pact between the ecclesiastical authorities and the Senate of Palermo, ratified by Clement VIII, whereby stole fees in that territory were abolished because of widespread abuse, the civil authorities having agreed to endow the various parishes deprived of this source of income.[61]

Although there is an intimate relation between the pastor's obligation to administer the sacraments and sacramentals and his right to receive the stole fees attached to them, they are in themselves juridically separate entities, and the former can exist independently of the latter. Against those who are unable to make an offering, the right to stole fees cannot be urged; nevertheless, in accordance with the counsel of the Apostle Matthew,[62] which has been repeated innumerable times in the conciliar enactments of the last fifteen hundred years, canon 463, §4, forbids pastors to deny their ministry to such members of the faithful. Canonists who comment on this passage content themselves with quoting the words of the Code. The fact that they draw no parallel with the norms for determining the capacity of the faithful to pay fees for dispensations and so on, is in itself sufficient indication that no parallel exists. They leave the matter, as does the Code, to the prudent judgment and the common sense of the pastors. Circumstances vary so widely in particular cases that a general norm, even if it were possible to evolve one, would be useless. For example, a man who owns his own home is anything but a pauper, but if he has been without work for a considerable time and has consumed his other resources, he can hardly be expected to mortgage his home in order to make a baptismal offering. On the other hand,

---

[60] *L. c.*

[61] Cf. S. C. C., in *Panormitana*, 16 May, 1925—*AAS*, XVIII (1926), 10.

[62] "Gratis accepistis, gratis date": X, 8.

if a couple go to considerable expense to produce an extravagant wedding celebration, the pastor can hardly be expected to take their word for it if they tell him that they are unable to make an offering that is of obligation.

In particular cases, then, when the question of enforcing his rights arises, a pastor must not too readily invoke the redress prescribed against recusants in canon 2349; too great insistence on his title to such fees may embitter others of his flock besides those involved, and may even deprive religious weaklings of what little faith they have. The distinction between those who are unwilling to fulfill their obligation and those who are unable to do so is patent, and there is ordinarily little difficulty in determining when there is question of canon 2349 and when of canon 463, §4; in the relatively few cases that give rise to this difficulty, the presumption should be for the latter.

§6. *Ministers Other Than the Proper Pastor.*—It is pertinent to remark here that the right to assist at parochial functions, and consequently to receive stole fees when these are attached to them, is open to prescription, since neither the nature of this right nor ecclesiastical law forbids this.[63] Acquisitive prescription of this nature may be either privative or cumulative; by the former, one church or pastor acquires the exclusive right to functions ordinarily pertaining to another; by cumulative prescription a pastor acquires a right equivalent to that of the proper pastor to assist at such functions reserved to the latter as have been prescribed.[64] When, therefore, a pastor by virtue of either title just mentioned assists at functions which according to common law belong to another pastor, he may receive the stole fees attached to them, and is under no obligation to refund them to the proper pastor.

Ordinarily, however, when another assists at a function that is reserved to the pastor, the latter is entitled to the

[63] S. R. Rota, in *Salutarium*, 1 Jul. 1913—*AAS*, VI (1914), 46-48; in *Nucerina Paganorum*, 27 Jul. 1914—*AAS*, VII (1915), 189-190; Reiffenstuel, *Ius Canon. Univers.*, lib. II, tit. XXVI, n. 34; Engel *Colleg. Univers. Jur. Canon.*, lib. III, tit. XXIX, n. 5; Bouix, *De Paroch.*, Pars IV, cap. IX, §1, qu. 2, 2°.

[64] S. R. Rota, in *Salutarium*, 1 Jul. 1913—*AAS*, VI (1914), 46-48.

stole fees,[65] since he has an intention founded in law, not only to assist at all parochial functions,[66] but also to receive the offerings made at them.[67]

There are four occasions that commonly occur wherein a minister other than the proper pastor officiates at a parochial function. The first is when a priest assists outside the case of necessity and without the permission of the proper pastor. In this instance there exists no title whatever to justify the recipient in retaining the fee and he is obliged to refund it. The second is when the pastor, because of absence or some other reason, delegates another priest to assist in his place; the delegate in this case does not thereby acquire the right to retain the stole fees unless this was agreed upon in the arrangements which were made for his recompense. Again, for reasons of friendship, consanguinity and so on, a priest may assist at a parochial function with the permission of the proper pastor. Out of courtesy pastors often grant such permission, but in so doing they do not necessarily waive their right to receive the fees attached to these functions. There are two rights involved in the last two hypotheses: first, the right to assist at a parochial function; secondly, the right to receive the stole fee. While the second of these follows from the first, they are not so intimately united that they cannot be separated. Permission or delegation to assist is not a sufficiently conclusive indication of the pastor's mind to justify the one who officiates in retaining the fee, nor is the fact that the pastor does not demand it; and the presumption to the contrary would seem to be more presumptious than reasonable.

Finally, there is the case when another priest assists in necessity, when there is no possibility of securing either the proper pastor or his permission. The few authors who treat this phase of the subject say that the one who acts may retain the stole fee since necessity makes him the

---

[65] Can. 463, §3; Ojetti, *Synopsis*, v. *Jura Stolae*, n. 2554; Bouix, *De Parocho*, Pars IV, cap. IX, §1, qu. 2, 1°

[66] S. R. Rota, in *Theatina*, 23 Mar. 1911—*AAS*, III (1911), 425.

[67] S. C. C., in *Lucana*, 17 Dec. 1904—*ASS*, XXXVII, 697.

pastor's agent in this instance. This opinion may be followed in practice, since the authority of those who propose it makes it extrinsically probable. Moreover, if it were observed by all it would cause little or but slight injustice, not only because such cases are relatively few, but also because the circumstance of necessity is likely to favor a pastor as often as it prejudices his rights. Nevertheless, the arguments against this view and in favor of the pastor's right to receive the fee even when necessity makes another the minister would appear to be equally convincing. In the first place, to say that the minister is entitled to the fee because he takes the pastor's place, that is, because he assists, is almost equivalent to saying that he is entitled to the fee for assisting. In other words, this view would seem to make the fee tantamount to remuneration for assistance at the function. This not only savors slightly of simony, but it is apparently opposed to the very theory of stole fees. These offerings are not given in recompense for the sacraments or sacramentals administered, nor, as one theory of Mass stipends proposes, are they remuneration for the labor involved in assisting at a function; rather, they are offered on these occasions, solely in recognition of the constant care involved in ministering to the spiritual needs of the faithful, and as a contribution towards the sustenance of the one who exercises that care. To say, then, that the minister of Baptism in a case of necessity, for example, may retain the baptismal offering, is to entitle him to what is offered in gratitude for, and in recognition of, attention to all the spiritual necessities of the one baptized, which, in the event the person lives, will devolve, not on the one who administered Baptism, but on the proper pastor of the one baptized.

Theoretically, therefore, it would seem that offerings must be ceded to the proper pastor, even when another acts from necessity. Practically, as was asserted above, there is no obligation to follow this. As a matter of fact, not only in case of necessity, but in other instances wherein common law permits others to assist without securing the pastor's permission, the obligation to refund the fee cannot be urged. These will be mentioned in the treatment of the fees attached to such functions.

In all cases of illicit assistance, the fee to be restored to the proper pastor must be equivalent to that which is in force in his diocese,[68] since that is the amount which he would have received had no one usurped his right. It would seem that this is true, even though there be no fee, or but a small one, attached to the function in the place where it took place; the intention of the principle of justice involved here is evidently to repair the injury to the pastor, as well as to prevent the minister from profiting by an illicit act. If, however, the one who assists acts with the permission of the proper pastor, there is no obligation on the part of the minister to make up the difference between what is offered and the fee to which the proper pastor is ordinarily entitled; and if nothing is given, there need be no restitution whatever. The reason for this is that if he acts with permission there is no intention to defraud, and the fact of permission is in itself sufficient to nullify any obligation of restitution.[69]

§7. *The Fees for Masses Reserved to the Pastor.*—When a priest, other than the pastor, celebrates a nuptial or funeral Mass, which are reserved to the pastor because they involve parochial functions, the question arises whether the offering for the Mass is to be divided, or must it be conceded integrally to the celebrant. It is necessary, first of all, to determine whether the celebrant was permitted or committed to say the Mass. If for personal reasons he secured the pastor's permission to celebrate, then, either by custom or from gratitude for the latter's courtesy, he generally foregoes his right to the stipend.[70]

When the pastor commits such a Mass to another priest, however, other circumstances must be considered. Wherever custom or statute states that the larger stipend for nuptial or exequial Masses is due because of the labor, singing, and unusual hour such Masses ordinarily involve,

[68] Augustine, *Commentary*, II, p. 542.

[69] Reg. 27, Reg. Jur., in VI°.

[70] Keller, *Mass Stipends*, p. 139.

this must be given to the celebrant in its entirety; but where the same authorities decide that the larger stipend for such Masses is intended to comprehend also a stole fee, the pastor is entitled to what is given over and above the stipend for the type of Mass (*lecta* or *cantata*) celebrated, and the latter is due to the celebrant.[71] When the offering exceeds the amount which custom or statute decrees for nuptial or exequial Masses, the pastor may retain the surplus as a stole fee,[72] even in an instance where these authorities award him part of the usual offering under the same title.

§8. *The Donor's Intention.*—Another question that arises when a priest other than the pastor assists at a function reserved to the latter is the disposal of that part of the offering in excess of the determined fee, supposing, of course, that more than is required by statute or custom is given. Whether or not the one who assisted had permission to do so,[73] the fee itself belongs to the pastor, and he is likewise entitled to the sum which is in excess of the stated fee unless it is certain that the donor intended the one who assisted to receive it.[74] This clause of the law explicitly acknowledges the right of the donor to dispose of any part of his offering which exceeds the amount that is of obligation, and particular laws which implicitly or explicitly deny this right by determining the destination of both the fee and the excess are hereby abrogated.[75] The pastor's right to receive what is assigned to him, however, is of primary consideration. Even if the donor expressly gives his offering to the one who assists, his obligation towards the pastor nullifies this intention regarding the

---

[71] S. C. C., in *Colonien.*, 25 Jul. 1874, ad 2um—*ASS*, VIII, 84; in *Treviren.*, 11 May 1888, ad 2um—Gasparri, *De Eucharistia*, I, n. 603; *Le Canoniste Contemporaine*, XII (1889), 399-407; *Nouvelle Revue Theologique*, XXI (1889), 229-244; *Irish Eccl. Record*, XXXIII (1929), 65-67 & 406-408; Ojetti, *Synopsis*, v. *Jura Stolae*, n. 2554; Cappello, *De Sacramentis*, I, n. 704; Bargilliat, *Praelectiones J. C.*, II, n. 1120, b).

[72] Vermeersch-Creusen, *Epitome*, II, n. 108, 3.

[73] Augustine, *Commentary on Canon Law*, II, p. 542; Ayrinhac, *Constitution of the Church*, n. 273.

[74] Can. 463, §3.

[75] Can. 6, 1°.

amount that is due to the pastor; and only to that part of the offering which exceeds the usual fee can his intention be applied.[76]

The law demands that the one who assists be *certain* that the excess was intended for him before he can retain it. The rules for determining this are the same as those used ordinarily to ascertain the "*intuitu personae*" of Mass stipends. The excess may be kept if it is given because of the dignity, office, poverty, etc., of the one who assists, or because of friendship or gratitude.[77] This intention, however, is not too readily to be presumed, but must be determined either expressly or from other unequivocal indications.[78] Whether he assists licitly or illicitly does not affect the minister's right to retain the surplus, provided only that he is morally certain it was intended for him.

Article II.—The Ownership of Stole Fees

§1. *Ordinary Dominium.*—The pastor's dominium or ownership of stole fees, like other phases of this subject, has undergone considerable change with the course of time. For centuries after the period when the economic policy of the Church first assigned parishes their own revenues, pastors enjoyed practically perfect dominium over such offerings. When their income from other sources was insufficient to support them, they were of necessity compelled to use this revenue for that purpose, but they were at liberty to dispose of the surplus in this instance, or of the whole amount in the event that other revenues insured their support, in whatever manner they saw fit. One restriction to the otherwise free disposition of this property is mentioned by Gasquet,[79] who says that unreasonable extravagance and ostentation in "squandering such ecclesiastical revenues" was probably reprehensible, in so far as it might prove injurious to the devotion of the faithful which prompted such offerings. As is evident, however, this re-

[76] *Amer. Eccl. Rev.*, LXX (1924), pp. 526-527.

[77] Gasparri, *De Eucharistia*, I, n. 606; *Le Canoniste Contemporaine*, XII (1889), 407.

[78] S. C. C., in *Colonien.*, 25 Jul. 1874—*ASS*, VIII, 83.

[79] *Parish Life in Mediæval England*, p. 10.

striction proceeded, not from any defect in the nature of the dominium itself, but from the necessity of preserving this right of the parochial office by avoiding that which might jeopardize it.

In comparatively recent years considerable change has occurred in this respect, so that at present there is a lack of uniformity throughout the Church in the status of dominial rights over stole fees. In some dioceses such offerings are the exclusive property of the pastor; in others the assistants of the parish are entitled to share in them; finally, in not a few territories, the pastor is merely the custodian and administrator of stole fees. In the last instance they are applied, it is true, to defray the expenses of clerical sustentation, but their administration is so defined by statute that the subjective liberty of disposition which is always associated with true and perfect dominium is necessarily excluded.

The statutes of provincial councils and diocesan synods were the agents which effected this change. The reasons to which they can be assigned were chiefly two: first, the utility of the diocese and the necessity of alleviating the financial burden of the faithful;[80] and second, to avoid disputes and dissension among the parochial clergy by an equitable distribution of these offerings.[81] There is nothing

[80] Cf. II Prov. Synod of Westminster, 1855, n. 15 (Mansi, XLVII, 275-276): "As to the application of money derived from stole fees, there is no uniform practice throughout the whole Church . . . . The proceeds derived from this source should be ordinarily considered as belonging to the priests; though they are distributed in different ways, in different places. That distribution seems to be the best, which is most conducive to alleviate the burthen of the mission." Translation from Guy, *The Synods in English*, p. 162.

[81] Cf. II Plen. Council of Baltimore, 1866, *Acta et Decreta*, n. 94: "Lest a lust of filthy lucre should infect the sacerdotal order, or dissensions arise among priests living together on account of the alms freely offered by the faithful in the administration of baptism and marriage, we admonish bishops to establish in their next synod, or otherwise, with the advice of their priests, an equitable way of distributing these offerings among the priests residing in the same house, also taking into consideration the chief claim as well as the graver duties of the pastor." Translation from Smith, *Notes on the Second Plenary Council of Baltimore*, p. 83.

to be gained by discussing the question of dominium where stole fees are regulated in such a way that the pastor has only the administration of this revenue along certain definite and determined lines; but where they are assigned to pastors and their assistants without restrictions or regulations of any kind regarding the disposal of this income, they acquire full and perfect dominium over it. In this instance the following facts are pertinent.

Money that is acquired on the occasion and by reason of sacerdotal functions is considered quasi-patrimonial property;[82] this is the common opinion among canonists,[83] although some have regarded it as ecclesiastical property and consequently subjected it to the restrictions governing the administration and disposal of such goods. The latter opinion is practically abandoned now and juridically this property has the same status as the *"peculium quasi-castrense"* of Roman Law.[84] Clerics enjoy full and perfect dominium over it;[85] they can apply and dispose of it as they see fit,[86] either while living, or by testament, after death,[87] since their ownership is restricted neither by law, nor by the express or tacit will of the faithful making the offerings.[88] If they are possessed of such quasi-patrimonial

[82] Pirhing, *Canonum Doctrina,* lib. III, tit. XXV, proem; Ojetti, *Synopsis,* v. *Patrimonialia Bona,* n. 3069; Soglia, *Inst. Jur. Priv. Eccl.,* lib. II, cap. IV, n. 119; Pichler, *Epitome J. C.,* lib. III, tit. XXV, 1; Carriere, *De Justitia et Jure,* n. 182; S. Poenitentiaria, 9 Aug. 1821 et 9 Jan. 1823 (apud Carriere, *op. cit.,* n. 194).

[83] Reiffenstuel, *Ius Canon. Univers.,* lib. III, tit. XXV, n. 7.

[84] Pirhing, *Canonum Doctrina,* lib. III, tit. XXV, proem. "Under Constantine came the *peculium quasi-castrense*: whatever the son made as a civil servant was his own property, except that he could not dispose of it by will, a privilege only conferred by Justinian. Subsequently this peculium came to embrace everything the son earned in a professional capacity."—Leage, *Roman Private Law,* p. 79.

[85] Ojetti, *Synopsis,* v. *Patrimonialia Bona,* n. 3069.

[86] Bened. XIV, *De Beatif. Servor. Dei,* lib. III, cap. XXXIV, n. 23 (*Opera Omnia,* III, 536); Pirhing, *Canonum Doctrina,* lib. III, tit. XXV, 1; S. Poenitentiaria, 9 Jan. 1823 (apud Carriere, *De Justitia et Jure,* n. 194).

[87] C. 9, X, *de testament.,* III, 26.

[88] Soglia, *Inst. Jur. Priv. Eccl.,* lib. II, cap. IV, n. 119; Pichler *Epitome J. C.,* lib. III, tit. XXV, n. 1; Carriere, *op. cit.,* n. 182.

property and die intestate, their legitimate heirs inherit it.[89]

Although it is evident from this summary that there is no legal impediment to the free exercise of this dominium, undue extravagance in the expenditure of the revenue from stole fees is undoubtedly reprehensible, not only for the reason alleged above by Gasquet, but also for another, the obligation of avoiding scandal and of observing clerical modesty.[90] To this necessity which affects all phases of clerical life, not even the perfect dominium of property is an exception.

Where a parish is confided to the care of a religious pastor and stole fees are assigned to him by custom or statute, the one to acquire dominium of them is determined according as certain hypotheses are verified. For one who is solemnly professed: if the Order to which he belongs can possess property, ownership of stole fees is vested in the Order itself, the province or the House, as the constitutions dispose; if not, the Holy See acquires dominium of them.[91] The same holds true for religious bound only by simple vows; since stole fees as such are given not *"intuitu personae,"* but rather for personal industry and by reason of title to the parochial office,[92] they are governed by canon 580, §2.

§2. *Stole Fees as Beneficial Dowry.*—The various items which can be used to endow a benefice are enumerated in canon 1410, and among them stole fees are mentioned. Ordinarily this income is not considered as part of the fruit of a benefice; in fact, before the Code it was disputed whether or not stole fees could constitute beneficial revenue.[93] That they can be employed for this end must now be admitted, but there is required the positive declaration of the Ordinary to that effect in erecting the benefice; since the enumeration of possible sources of revenue in canon 1410 is disjunctive, and not conjunctive, stole fees can be assimilated to the beneficial dowry only when truly

[89] Soglia, *l. c.*

[90] Genicot, *Theol. Moral. Inst.*, I, n. 475.

[91] Can. 582.

[92] Carriere, *De Justitia et Jure*, n. 182.

[93] Golden, *Parochial Benefices in the New Code*, p. 10.

ecclesiastical property is unavailable or insufficient to constitute it.[94] When once they have been so applied, however, they remain permanently attached to the beneficial office.[95]

When stole fees are considered part of the beneficial dowry, anything offered voluntarily by the faithful that is over and above what custom or statute demands need not be ceded to the benefice,[96] but may be retained by the pastor, whether or not this excess was offered to him *"intuitu personae."* The reason for this is evident: it is to the pastor's disadvantage to constitute stole fees as part of the dowry;[97] hence, it is both legitimate and proper to restrict the interpretation of the words of the canon—"within the limits of diocesan taxation or legitimate custom"—to the literal sense. The amount determined by these authorities is all that is certain; only that amount can legitimately be estimated in computing and constituting the dowry, and therefore, it is only that amount to which the benefice is strictly entitled.

The same canon that settled the controversy as to whether or not stole fees could constitute part of a beneficial dowry, gave rise to another equally important dispute. Canon 1473 imposes an obligation on beneficiaries to give to the poor or to pious causes whatever revenue derived from their benefices they do not spend for their own support. This is one of the stipulations that govern the disposal of strictly ecclesiastical property, under which beneficial income is classified.[98] When, therefore, stole fees constitute part of the dowry of a benefice, the question arises: are they subject to the impediments that hinder the free disposal of ecclesiastical goods, or do they retain the legal status of quasi-patrimonial property and pass to the perfect dominium of the beneficiary.

---

[94] Vermeersch-Creusen, *Epitome,* II, n. 798; Vromant, *De Bonis Eccl. Temporal.,* n. 24, nota (3).

[95] Can. 1409; cf. Augustine, *Commentary on Çanon Law,* VI, p. 495; Vromant, *l. c.*

[96] Vermeersch-Creusen, *op. cit.,* n. 743.

[97] At least according to one view of the legal status of such property, to which attention is given in the ensuing paragraphs.

[98] Cf. Ojetti, *Synopsis,* v. *Bona,* n. 654.

Aertnys leaves the matter in doubt.[99] Another opinion, considering only the relation between canons 1410 and 1473, and prescinding from other aspects of stole fees, declares that they are ecclesiastical property and must be administered like any other beneficial income.[100] Vermeersch-Creusen holds a more liberal and, it would seem, a more logical view of the question, contending that even when they constitute a part of the beneficial dowry, the beneficiary is under no positive obligation to distribute the surplus to pious causes.[101] The reason alleged is that the opposite opinion presupposes an odious correction of the law, a new evil or prejudice; and without the express declaration of the legislator, a disposition of the law intended merely to facilitate the constitution of a benefice is insufficient to justify this presumption. Stole fees, as was asserted in the preceding section, have by nature the legal status of quasi-patrimonial property; the fact that, by exception, the legislator permits them to be listed among the revenues of a benefice, if by so doing a dowry can be legitimately constituted where this would otherwise be impossible, is not sufficiently indicative of his intention to justify the conclusion that he thereby changes the legal status of this revenue. It is primarily beneficiaries who profit by the erection of benefices, and certainly it is more to their advantage to forget, or at least to distinguish, obsolete, pre-Code definitions, and to admit that the dowry of a benefice may now be composed of both strictly ecclesiastical and quasi-patrimonial property, rather than to contend that income which is naturally quasi-patrimonial is converted into purely ecclesiastical property by assimilation to a beneficial dowry, and to demand that it be administered and disposed of as such.

[99] Theol. Moral., I, n. 662, IV; although he refuses to class them as quasi-patrimonial property in n. 661, 3°: "QUASI-PATRIMONIALIA, seu INDUSTRIALIA, quae acquirunt tamquam stipendium ob functiones sacras, sed non ex iis quae constituunt dotem beneficii."

[100] Bargilliat, *Droits et Devoirs des Cures*, n. 528, e).

[101] *Epitome*, II, n. 798; Vromant, *De Bonis Eccl. Temporal.*, n. 216, 3), b). Slater, "Property Rights of Parish Priests," *Amer. Eccl. Rev.*, LXII (1920), 548-550, holds the same view, although his arguments are less convincing.

CHAPTER IV

THE RIGHTS OF THE WHITE STOLE

Article I.—Baptismal Fees

The Code nowhere demands that an offering be made at any particular function; the canons that make mention of fees at marriages and funerals do so on the supposition that money is usually offered on these occasions,[1] and they have application only where such offerings are customary. For Baptism there is not even hypothetical mention of a fee, although the practice of making oblations at this function is almost universally observed. Fees on this occasion, therefore, are directly and immediately governed by the prescriptions of canon 463, in accordance with which all regulations for stole fees must ultimately be orientated. What was asserted above in the commentary on this canon is applicable here, for the administration of solemn Baptism is a strictly parochial function by common law, assistance at which is reserved to the proper pastor of the party to be baptized.[2]

The proper pastor for the Baptism of infants is the pastor of the place where the child's father has a domicile or quasi-domicile at the time of birth.[3] The pastor of the place of birth, if this be different from that of the father's domicile, does not thereby acquire the right to baptize the child.[4] Moreover, outside his own parish no pastor may

[1] *Irish Eccl. Record,* XXXIII (1929), 65.

[2] Cans. 462, 1° and 738, §1.

[3] Cans. 738, §1, 94, §1 and 93, §1. For illegitimate or posthumous children, the pastor of the mother's domicile or quasi-domicile has the right to baptize (c. 90, §1).

[4] Can. 738, §2. A custom to the contrary may be tolerated if it be a centenary custom. Cf. can. 5; Vermeersch-Creusen, *Epitome,* II, n. 23; Giraldi, Additio ad Barbosa, *De Offic. et Pot. Paroch.,* Pars II, cap. XVIII, n. 7.

confer solemn Baptism without the permission of the pastor whose territorial rights are involved, even though the one to be baptized is subject to his jurisdiction by reason of domicile or quasi-domicile;[5] nor may a pastor in his own parish baptize solemnly the parishioners of another pastor, unless it is impossible to reach the proper pastor without inconvenience and delay.[6]

Inconvenience is a relative term and, as it affects this question, varies according to the circumstances of person and place; it involves considerations of distance and accessibility, the physical capacity of the subject for Baptism, the financial status of the parents, and so on. General rules to define this inconvenience—and diocesan statutes which determine it are entirely legitimate[7]—are usually estimated on distance alone; consequently they are often inequitable, but would seem to be justified by the fact that they eliminate dissension and disputes. Where it is not defined by statute, common law leaves it to the prudence of pastors to consider the circumstances peculiar to each case, and to determine with common sense and without cupidity what is most consonant with justice to all concerned. The delay at issue undoubtedly refers to the necessity of conferring this sacrament on infants as soon as possible; this is stressed in canon 770. The "*quamprimum*" of this canon is variously interpreted; it is generally admitted, however, that a delay of more than a month without sufficient reason constitutes a grave infraction of the law.[8] Diocesan statutes may likewise determine the maximum time within which this sacrament must be administered, and while they may legitimately specify a time that is less than a month, they may not extend this interpretation of

---

[5] Can. 739.

[6] Can. 738, §2.

[7] Vermeersch-Creusen, *Epitome,* II, n. 23.

[8] Vermeersch-Creusen, *Epitome,* II, n. 52; Cappello, *De Sacramentis,* I, n. 149, 1°. For a more detailed interpretation of this interval, see Chapter VI.

common law by admitting a delay in excess of that time.[9] It is to be noted that the conditions of inconvenience and delay must be verified simultaneously; if it is foreseen that the inconvenience will cease to exist before the time-limit for conferring Baptism elapses, no one may infringe the rights of the proper pastor to administer the sacrament.

Without these conditions to justify his action, therefore, it is gravely reprehensible for any pastor to baptize the subject of another pastor,[10] and he is bound to restore the stole fee to the pastor whose right he has usurped. This, of course, does not apply when there is question of necessity. Even in this instance, however, the proper pastor must be preferred to others if it is possible to reach him; otherwise there is no justification for insisting on parochial rights, and any pastor may confer the sacrament and retain the fee as though it were merely a sacerdotal function.[11]

With the concepts of inconvenience and delay given above, it is possible to solve the question of restitution which the two cases previously mentioned involve. In the first case, where one pastor violates the territorial rights of another in behalf of his own subject, if the child could have been brought to its proper church within the time allowed he is entitled to retain the fee, since the pastor of the place acquired no right to baptize it. The fact that he is guilty of a serious infringement of parochial rights, while gravely reprehensible, does not in itself imply an obligation of restitution, for the latter is founded on the right to assist, and that right is evidently his. On the other hand, where it would necessitate considerable inconvenience to take the child to its proper church within the time allotted, the conditions of the second case are verified, and the pastor of

---

[9] Vermeersch-Creusen, *l. c.;* Cappello, *l. c.*

[10] II Plen. Council of Balt., 1866, *Acta et Decreta*, n. 227.

[11] When, however, such Baptism of necessity is conferred in the proper church of the subject, the pastor is entitled to the fee irrespective of whether he or another assists, since canon 463, §3 makes no distinction.

the parish where the child is actually staying[12] receives jurisdiction from common law to confer Baptism, and consequently to receive and retain the stole fee.[13] If the proper pastor of the child baptizes it under these circumstances, he is obliged to restore the fee to the pastor of the parish where the child is staying, since the conditions of inconvenience and delay give the latter the exclusive right to confer the sacrament.

Any pastor in his own church may baptize those who have nowhere a proper pastor by reason of parochial domicile or quasi-domicile. By virtue of canon 94, §2 and §3, it is necessary that they be temporarily resident in his parish, that is, at the time they present themselves or their children for baptism.[14] For those who have more than one canonical residence, the pastor of quasi-domicile is equally competent to assist with the pastor of domicile,[15] so that where there is more than one proper pastor the one to be baptized, or his parents, may choose one of them at will, irrespective of where birth occurs, since all have an equal right to assist. Where a question of restitution involves a plurality of proper pastors, it would seem legitimate and wise to follow an analogy with the return of the parochial portion. If, therefore, the child is born in one of its proper parishes and is illicitly baptized elsewhere, it would seem that the fee should be returned to the pastor of the parish where birth occurred. If the child is born outside its proper parishes and is baptized illicitly because the conditions of inconvenience and delay are not present, it would

---

[12] In their literal sense, the words of canon 738, §2, ". . . quilibet parochus in suo territorio . . .", would permit any nearby pastor to whom the child is presented to baptize it licitly; however, by analogy with the proper pastor for funerals, when transfer of the body to its proper parish is inconvenient, it would seem that they should be restricted to mean only the pastor of the parish where the child is actually staying.

[13] Can. 738, §2. Cf. Woywod, *Practical Commentary*, I, n. 633; *Irish Eccl. Record*, XXIII (1924), 527.

[14] Formerly they were free to be baptised wherever they wished: S. Alphonsus, *Theol. Moral.*, lib. VI, n. 114.

[15] Can. 94, §1.

seem that the fees should be returned to, and divided equally among, all and only those of its proper parishes to which it could have been brought conveniently and within the proper time for conferring the sacrament.

The proper pastor for the baptism of converts is the pastor of the parish within whose limits they live.[16] However, particular law or legitimate custom may derogate from common law on this point, and where either of these authorities decrees that the pastor who instructs the party is entitled to assist at Baptism, he may retain the fee.[17]

In some places a church may enjoy what is termed a cumulative right to baptize;[18] this right entitles the pastor of such a church to baptize all who present themselves or their charges to him for that purpose, even though they belong to another parish, provided only that they have a domicile or quasi-domicile within the territory or city over which this right extends. Since this is an acquired right, it is not lost by the Code's injunction that every parish church must have its own baptismal font.[19] In interpreting this right, the Pontifical Commission for the Interpretation of the Code declared recently: that churches which enjoyed an exclusive right to baptize before the Code have now only a cumulative right; that the cumulative right to baptize cannot be acquired by any church in the future; and finally, that an existing cumulative right extends also over the subjects of newly erected parishes, provided these be within the proper territorial or city limits.[20]

Article II.—Matrimonial Fees

Canon 1097.—§1. Parochus autem vel loci Ordinarius matrimonio licite assistunt:

1° . . .

---

16 Ferraris, v. *Baptismus*, Art. IV, n. 17; Giraldi, Additio ad Barbosa, *De Offic. et Pot. Paroch.*, Pars II, cap. XVIII, n. 17.

17 Cf. Synod. Dioeces. S. Ludovici VII, 1929, n. 53.

18 Can. 774, §1; juridically called the "*jus fontis* [*baptismalis*] *cumulativum.*"

19 *Ibid.*

20 12 Nov. 1922, ad IV—*AAS*, XIV (1922), 662.

2° Constito insuper de domicilio vel quasi-domicilio vel menstrua commoratione aut, si de vago agatur, actuali commoratione alterutrius contrahentis in loco matrimonii;

3° Habita, si conditiones deficiant de quibus n. 2, licentia parochi vel Ordinarii domicilii vel quasi-domicilii aut menstruae commorationis alterutrius contrahentis, nisi vel de vagis actu itinerantibus res sit, qui nullibi commorationis sedem habent, vel gravis necessitas intercedat quae a licentia petenda excuset.

§2. In quolibet casu pro regula habeatur ut matrimonium coram sponsae parocho celebretur, nisi iusta causa excuset; matrimonia autem catholicorum mixti ritus, nisi aliud particulari iure cautum sit, in ritu viri et coram eiusdem parocho sunt celebranda.

§3. Parochus qui sine licentia iure requisita matrimonio assistit, emolumenta stolae non facit sua, eaque proprio contrahentium parocho remittat.

§1. *Residence and Marriage.*—Assistance at marriage and the imparting of the solemn nuptial blessing are parochial functions reserved to the pastor by canon 462, 4°. Ordinarily speaking, the proper pastor for parochial functions is to be determined by domicile or quasi-domicile. Canon 1097, however, which enumerates those who are qualified to assist licitly at the celebration of marriage, authorizes the pastor of monthly residence also to act; so that for this function his right to assist is equivalent to that of the pastor of domicile or quasi-domicile.

Anyone sufficiently acquainted with the history of marriage legislation will admit that it is difficult to overrate the importance of residence in its relation to this sacrament. The fundamental changes in the form amply evidence this; although they resulted primarily from the necessity of safeguarding the validity of the sacrament, Church Law has been equally insistent and uncompromising in demanding the liceity of the minister's assistance. Prescinding from the influence and effects of impediments, the validity of marriage under existing legislation depends exclusively on territorial jurisdiction; on the other hand, the liceity of the sacrament and of the minister's assistance—

which alone entitles him to retain the stole fee[21]—is primarily a question of personal jurisdiction, which in turn hinges on the place and quality of residence of either party to the marriage contract. For this reason, and for others, namely, because change of residence is frequently antecedent to or concomitant with marriage, and because residence in such cases is often affected and some times nullified when made with a view to marriage and informed by that intention, it is necessary to consider what constitutes domicile, quasi-domicile and monthly residence, and how they may be acquired, retained and lost.

When domicile or quasi-domicile is acquired merely through a residence that is protracted for the space of time legitimately required to constitute it, there is no doubt as to its existence. When, however, it is desired to establish domicile or quasi-domicile at the beginning of residence by virtue of the intention of remaining for the time required, the existence of either must not be presumed without sufficient evidence. Merely legal tenure of property without inhabiting it is, of course, insufficient to institute domicile;[22] it does not even constitute the element of residence unless it is accompanied by some form of domestic life. In addition, the intention which informs the act of residence to make of it either domicile or quasi-domicile must be efficacious to produce this effect immediately. Conditional intentions may or may not do this: if the condition is resolutive —as is the "*si nihil inde avocet*" of canon 92, §1 and §2— the intention is unimpeded; but when the condition is suspensory—as is the case when residence is acquired solely in anticipation of marriage—the effect of the intention is contingent upon the fulfillment of that condition.[23] In this case, since domicile does not exist until the moment the marriage has taken place, the pastor of the place of mere

---

[21] Can. 1097, §3.

[22] S. R. Rota, in *Parisien.*, 24 Mar. 1911—*AAS*, III (1911), 326.

[23] Maroto, *Instit. Jur. Canon.*, I, n. 411, 1ª, footnote (3). "The unanimous view of Canonists who have discussed the point is that an intention which has a suspensory condition attached to it is of no avail for securing a domicile until the condition is actually fulfilled": Farren, *Domicile and Quasi-Domicile*, p. 75.

residence is not entitled to assist licitly in anticipation of the personal jurisdiction which he will then secure.

According to a principle of Roman law, affianced women did not change their domicile before the marriage contract.[24] This was accepted and applied in ecclesiastical jurisprudence;[25] there is therefore a presumption of law against the existence of such domiciles based on the fact that they are apparently acquired solely with a view to marriage. The Code demands that all under twenty-one years of age must necessarily retain the domicile of their parents or guardians,[26] but since they may legitimately acquire their proper quasi-domicile, it would seem logical to apply the above presumption to any such residence they may locate within several months before marriage, or at least between engagement and marriage.[27] This presumption in no way prejudices their right to acquire a quasi-domicile, since it necessarily yields to proof that residence was not acquired in anticipation of marriage.

A domicile or quasi-domicile, when it is once legitimately established, is regarded as an acquired right;[28] long continued absence is in itself insufficient to deprive one of it.[29] Mere tenure of a home, though inadequate to institute domicile, is often sufficient to prove the existence of one that is already acquired,[30] and the moral continuity of quasi-domicile very probably persists even though one be absent

---

[24] Dig. L, i, 32: "Ea quae desponsa est, ante contractas nuptias suum non mutat domicilium."

[25] S. C. C., in *Parisien.*, 28 Jan. 1899—*ASS*, XXXII, 390; S. R. Rota, in *Mohilovien.*, 27 Jul. 1915—*AAS*, VIII, 82; in *Parisien*, 5 May 1914—*AAS*, VI (1914), 397; in *Parisien*, 27 Jan. 1912—*AAS*, IV (1912), 282.

[26] Can. 93, §1.

[27] Since it refers only to the intention, monthly residence and quasi-domicile that is actually protracted for the space of six months are not affected by this presumption.

[28] S. R. Rota, in *Gratianopolitana*, 17 Jul. 1911—*AAS*, IV (1912), 677.

[29] S. R. Rota, in *Ravennatense*, 15 May 1911—*AAS*, III (1911), 483.

[30] S. R. Rota, in *Gratianopolitana*, cited in note 28.

repeatedly over the week-end.[31] Moreover, the necessary or legal domicile which minors share with their parents or guardians becomes their own proper domicile when they reach the age of twenty-one, and by a presumption of law they retain it even though they may actually live elsewhere,[32] since the acquisition of a new domicile of itself does not prove the loss of one already acquired.[33]

The loss of domicile or quasi-domicile, on the other hand, is regarded as something odious;[34] it is more easily retained than lost, since its tenure is considered advantageous, and in doubt the presumption is in favor of its existence.[35] Ordinarily it is lost only through the destruction of the two causes which established it, that is to say, by actual departure with the intention of not returning;[36] moreover, if the intention not to return is dependent on a suspensory condition, like the intention to acquire domicile it is of no avail until the condition is fulfilled.[37] Children who have attained their majority, however, lose their parental or family domicile if while they are absent from it the parental domicile is changed to another parish; to regain the new domicile with their parents or guardians requires the same conditions that are necessary to acquire any domicile or quasi-domicile.[38] A wife, too, loses her proper domicile and acquires that of her husband,[39] but

[31] Farren, *Domicile and Quasi-Domicile*, p. 91; *Amer. Eccl. Rev.*, LXXIV (1926), 533.

[32] S. R. Rota, in *Parisien*, 27 Jan. 1912—*AAS*, IV (1912), 285; 4 Mar. 1916—*AAS*, VIII (1916), 370.

[33] S. R. Rota, in *Gratianopolitana*, 17 Jul. 1911—*AAS*, IV (1912), 680.

[34] S. R. Rota, in *Gratianopolitana*, 8 Apr. 1913—*AAS*, V (1913), 354; in *Parisien*, 4 Mar. 1916—*AAS*, VIII (1916), 370; *Irish Eccl. Record*, XXVI (1925), pp. 627-628.

[35] S. R. Rota, in *Parisien*, 4 Mar. 1916—*AAS*, VIII (1916), 370.

[36] S. R. Rota, in *Gratianopolitana*, 17 Jul. 1911—*AAS*, IV (1912), 677; in *Parisien*, 4 Mar. 1916—*AAS*, VIII (1916), 369; *Irish Eccl. Record*, XXVI (1925), pp. 628-629. "Omnis res, per quascunque causas nascitur, per easdem dissolvitur."—c. 1, X, *de reg. jur.*, V, 41.

[37] Farren, *Domicile and Quasi-Domicile*, pp. 95-96.

[38] S. R. Rota, in *Parisien*, 27 Jan. 1912—*AAS*, IV (1912), 285-286.

[39] Can. 93, §1.

when domicile is lost through marriage, it is to be noted that it is marriage itself, and not the intention to marry, that effects this,[40] so that the competence of the bride's pastor ceases only *after* the marriage contract.[41]

Monthly residence is, as the term indicates, mere residence protracted for the space of one month; it involves no question of intention since it was introduced in order to obviate the necessity of investigating the intention required to establish quasi-domicile.[42] This does not mean that *any* monthly residence in the past suffices; it refers only to that which immediately precedes the celebration of marriage and which is morally continuous up to that moment.[43] The time is to be computed as it is found in the calendar: it is completed *after* the day of the ensuing month corresponding to that on which it began, or, if this has no corresponding day, after the last day of the month.[44] Canonists admit that absence during the day for the purpose of work, recreation, and so on, or even absence for a whole day if it occurs only once or twice, does not break the moral continuity of the month, nor need the time of absence be supplied.[45] They are reluctant to admit more than that, and from their wording of this concession,[46] as well as from

---

[40] Farren, *op. cit.*, p. 77.

[41] S. R. Rota, in *Mohilovien.*, 27 Jul. 1915—*AAS*, VIII (1916), 82.

[42] S. C. de Discipl. Sacr., "*Liceitatis Matrimonii*", 28 Jan. 1916—*AAS*, VIII (1916), 66.

[43] "Verum *in actu celebrationis matronii defuit haec menstrua* sponsae commoratio, id quod reddit illicitam celebrationem connubii in paroecia S. Etenim illa verba Decreti: *constito . . . de menstrua commoratione* non ita sunt intelligenda ut sufficiat quaelibet menstrua commoratio *quondam* habita. Tunc enim nupturientes haberent parochum proprium pro licita celebratione matrimonii ubicumque per mensem commorati fuissent quocumque vitae tempore, quo nihil est magis alienum a mente legislatoris. . .": S. C. de Discipl. Sacr., *ibidem*.

[44] Can. 34, §3. The first day is not computed unless it is complete, i.e., unless it starts with the preceding midnight.

[45] Wernz-Vidal, *Ius Canonicum*, V, n. 541; Vermeersch-Creusen, *Epitome*, II, n. 399; Fanfani, *De Jure Parochorum*, n. 309; Farrugia, *De Matrimonio*, n. 230; Rossi, *De Matrimonii Celebratione*, n. 56, 3°), footnote (77); Chelodi, *Jus Matrimoniale*, n. 134, b).

[46] "Unius aut alterius diei." Cf. authors in footnote 45.

the relative brevity of a month's residence, it would seem that an absence of two full days in succession is sufficient to break the moral continuity and necessitate a new start.[47]

Although it is possible to be without a domicile or quasi-domicile, this lack of stable residence, according to a principle of Roman Law [48] accepted in canonical jurisprudence, is considered "odious, extraordinary, and not lightly to be presumed." [49] There are two classes of people for whom a lack of fixed residence at the time of marriage can legitimately be admitted: those who are habitually without domicile or quasi-domicile, and who are called *vagi* in canon law; and those who are only temporarily and by accident without domicile or quasi-domicile, as when one domicile is relinquished with the intention of not returning and another has not yet been acquired;[50] the latter are assimilated to, and for a time have the status of, *vagi*, although strictly speaking and by nature they are not such. It is noteworthy, also, that matrimonial legislation restricts the definition and application of the term *vagi* more than other fields of Church Law.[51] For them, as well as for those who possess a domicile or quasi-domicile, the month's residence mentioned above suffices to secure a proper pastor for marriage.[52]

§2. *The Right to the Fees.* With these ideas of canonical residence, references to the proper pastor for the celebration of marriage can be understood without serious difficulty. Canon 1097, §1, 2°, declares that the pastor of domi-

---

[47] ". . . menstrua commoratio praeterita, etiam ante paucos dies interrupta, nulli parocho quidquam iuris confert, . . .": Vermeersch-Creusen, *Epitome,* II, n. 399.

[48] Dig. L, 1, 27: "Difficile est sine domicilio esse quemquam."

[49] S. R. Rota, in *Parisien,* 27 Jan. 1912—*AAS,* IV (1912), 281; in *Parisien,* 5 May 1914—*AAS,* VI (1914), 399; in *Parisien,* 4 Mar. 1916—*AAS,* VIII (1916), 373-374.

[50] S. R. Rota, in *Parisien,* 5 May 1914, *ibidem.*

[51] Compare canons 91 and 1097, §1, 2° & 3°.

[52] S. C. Sacr., 12 Mar. 1910—*AAS,* II (1910), 193.

cile,[53] quasi-domicile or month's residence of either party to the marriage contract is entitled to assist licitly at its celebration. In a given instance, therefore, there may be a plurality of proper pastors competent to assist at the same marriage. Under these circumstances the parties to the contract may choose the one they prefer [54] to perform the ceremony with this restriction, that while the pastor of domicile or quasi-domicile may assist even though his subjects are actually residing elsewhere, the pastor of monthly residence can assist licitly only when at least one of the parties is dwelling in his parish, since the moral continuity of this residence must persist without notable interruption till the day of marriage. If one of the parties is a *vagus* and has some temporary abode at the time of marriage, the pastor of the place of abode is competent to assist licitly, even though the other contracting party has one or more proper pastors by reason of domicile, quasi-domicile or monthly residence.[55] If both the contracting parties are *vagi* and neither has even such a temporary abode, any pastor to whom they may present themselves is legitimately entitled to witness their marriage.[56] This would seem to be the only instance where the parties may choose any pastor they prefer without restrictions of any kind; the use of the plural number *"vagis"* is in marked distinction to the singular *"vago"* of canon 1097, §1, 2°, and to the *"alterutrius contrahentis"* of both 2° and 3°. This concession is, therefore, evidently taxative and restricted to the case where neither party to the contract has momentarily a dwelling place. In the event that only one of them is in such circumstances, the proper pastor of the other

---

[53] Or of any of the domiciles, if there be more than one. The possibility of this is admitted in: S. R. Rota, in *Gratianopolitana*, 8 Apr. 1913—*AAS*, V (1913), 345-346; in *Parisien*, 4 Mar. 1916—*AAS*, VIII (1916), 373-374; in *Ravennaten.*, 15 May 1911—*AAS*, III (1911) 486-487. The last decision declares that it is also possible to have two quasi-domiciles.

[54] Even one of the proper pastors of the groom for a just cause, of which more below.

[55] Can. 1097, §1, 2°.

[56] Can. 1097, §1, 3°.

party by reason of domicile, quasi-domicile, month's residence or, if another *vagus,* temporary residence, is entitled to assist.

In all the instances listed above, the pastor's competence to assist licitly is based on common law, and he is therefore entitled to receive and to retain the stole fees for such marriages. The same is true when he assists at marriage in grave necessity, even though he has no title to jurisdiction over the contracting parties, since grave necessity makes every pastor the proper pastor for this sacrament.[57] Not only when it is physically impossible to have the proper pastor of the contracting parties, but also whenever it is morally impossible or would involve serious inconvenience to secure his permission, the conditions for grave necessity are verified. It is generally admitted that it is sufficient to constitute grave necessity if there is likelihood that civil marriage may be attempted, or when immediate departure is imminent and necessary or when there is grave reason to conceal the marriage from the proper pastor.[58]

The Code directs that all marriages be celebrated before the pastor of the bride as a rule, unless a just cause excuses from observing this norm.[59] Whether or not this constitutes a true obligation is controverted.[60] That the obligation, if it exists, is not grave is evident both from the fact that the liceity of assistance for the groom's pastor is independent of the existence of a just cause, and because any just cause is sufficient to excuse from observing the rule.[61] Although this rule is undoubtedly intended to secure as just and equitable a distribution of the offerings

---

[57] Can. 1097, §1, 3°.

[58] Cf. Chelodi, *Jus Matrimoniale,* n. 135; De Smet, *Betrothment and Marriage,* I, n. 125, A; Wernz-Vidal, *Jus Canonicum,* V, n. 542.

[59] Can. 1097, §2.

[60] Cf. Chelodi, *l. c.;* Wernz-Vidal, *op. cit.,* V, n. 542, footnote (57).

[61] Since it is legitimate for particular law to demand more than common law, however, the statutes of diocesan synods or of provincial councils may define this obligation, or they may otherwise secure the evident end of the law by demanding that the offering made at marriage be given to the bride's pastor, irrespective of whether he or another assists at the ceremony.

made at marriage as is possible for all concerned, it cannot be urged that it implies an obligation on the part of the groom's pastor to refund the stole fee to the pastor of the bride, since the assistance of the former is always licit.

Any cause which is reasonable according to the criterion of common sense is sufficient to excuse the parties from the rule of celebrating marriage before the bride's pastor; this need not be grave. Hence relationship, friendship, prejudice, convenience or any other motive prompted by the desires and plans of the contracting parties is considered a just cause.[62]

When one of the parties is a non-Catholic, the pastor of the place where such a one has domicile, quasi-domicile or month's residence is competent to assist licitly at the marriage, since the law makes no distinction of religion.[63] The rule, therefore, directing that marriage be celebrated before the pastor of the bride holds good even though the latter be a non-Catholic. The fact of her religion, alone, however, would seem to constitute a just cause sufficient to excuse the parties from observing this rule if they desire to avail themselves of it.[64]

Unless particular law decrees otherwise, the pastor of the groom is to assist at the marriage of Catholics of mixed rite.[65] Despite the fact that this exception to the rule just mentioned is expressed in more emphatic language than the rule itself, since it is contained in the same paragraph and sentence, it would seem that the clause *"pro regula*

---

[62] Cf. Vlaming, *Praelect. Juris Matrim.*, II, n. 581, a, 1°; *Amer. Eccl. Rev.*, LXII (1920), 691.

[63] S. C. de Discipl. Sacr., *"Liceitatis Matrim."*, 28 Jan. 1916—*AAS*, VIII (1916), 65: ". . . Liquido patet sufficere, ad liceitatem, factum mere externum commorationis, praescindendo a facto conversionis sponsae in fidem catholicam. Porro voluntas legislatoris ex verbis legis petenda est iuxta illud effatum: *Legislator quod voluit expressit.* At in Decr. *Ne Temere* requiritur tantummodo menstrua commoratio alterutrius contrahentis, quin ullus sermo habeatur de eorumdem religione . . .". The same argument can be applied to the residence requirements of canon 1097, §1, 2° & 3°, since these also make no distinction of religion.

[64] Cf. *Amer. Eccl. Rev.*, LXII (1920), 691.

[65] Can. 1097, §2.

habeatur" may be applied to it also, and that there is no grave obligation either to abide by it or to restore the fee to the groom's pastor when the pastor of the bride assists. The particular law referred to is not to be understood in the ordinary sense of the term, i.e., diocesan or provincial law; it refers rather to the law of a particular rite, whether that law itself be universal or particular in its extension.[66]

In the event that the bride has more than one canonical residence and consequently more than one proper pastor for marriage, there is no definite rule of precedence which demands that the pastor of domicile be preferred to the pastor of quasi-domicile and so on. They are all equally competent to assist, as well as to retain the fee if they do so.

Whenever a pastor assists at marriage illicitly he is bound to return the stole fee to the proper pastor of the contracting parties.[67] If the parties belong to different parishes, since the rule in canon 1097, §2, was intended to regulate the equal distribution of matrimonial offerings, the fee should be returned to the pastor of the bride. And when the bride has more than one proper pastor by reason of domicile, quasi-domicile or month's residence, by analogy with canon 1236, §2, and because all were equally entitled to assist, the fee should be divided equally among her proper pastors.[68] Some authors deny that the pastor of month's residence is entitled to share in this restitution,[69] contending that he is not the proper pastor in the strict sense of the term. Others affirm his right to participate in the fee because, they say, restitution is founded on the

---

66 Cf. Decr. S. C. pro Eccl. Orient., 1 Mar. 1929, cap. IV, art. 39—*AAS*, XXI (1929), 159. This document states that marriages of the Greek-Ruthenians in the United States are to be regulated by the decree "*Ne Temere*"; when, therefore, they contract either among themselves or with Catholics of other rites, the pastor of the bride is to assist.

67 Can. 1097, §3.

68 Wernz-Vidal, *Ius Canonicum*, V, n. 542, footnote (58).

69 Cf. Cappello, *De Sacramentis*, III, n. 689, 5, c (citans Ojetti et Gennari).

right to assist.[70] The latter view would seem to be more correct. Even though the pastor of month's residence is not the proper pastor in the sense of canon 94, he is most certainly the proper pastor for matrimony, as the preceding paragraphs of canon 1097 clearly indicate; it is only logical then, to understand the third paragraph in the light of what precedes it. Moreover, if the pastor of month's residence is not entitled to restitution from one who assists illicitly, the purpose of canon 1097, §3, is frustrated in every instance where there is no question of domicile or quasi-domicile and the pastor of month's residence is alone competent to assist licitly.

As was asserted in the commentary on canon 463, the minister who from motives of friendship, relationship and so on secures the permission of the proper pastor to assist at marriage is not thereby entitled to retain the fee; canon 1097, §3, expressly obliges to restitution only those who assist illicitly, but the inference that all others may retain it is not sufficiently justified by the argument that they are here omitted. So, too, when the pastor deputes another to assist in his place, he is still entitled to receive the offering, and the delegate has a right only to what is agreed upon in the arrangements he makes with the pastor.

He is, of course, entitled to retain whatever is offered in excess of the usual fee, when it is certain that this is given to him *intuitu personae.* Moreover, when his assistance entails the celebration of a nuptial Mass, if custom or statute decrees that the whole offering is to be ceded to the celebrant, he is justified in retaining it; but where these same authorities decree that such an offering includes a stole fee, or when neither of these hypotheses is verified, he can retain only the amount determined or customary for the type of Mass celebrated.[71]

---

[70] Chelodi, *Jus Matrimoniale,* n. 135; Vlaming, *Praelectiones Juris Matrimonii.,* II, n. 583; Rossi, *De Matrimonii Celebratione,* n. 61; *Irish Eccl. Record,* XVII (1921), 624.

[71] Cf. Chapter III, art. I, §7.

CHAPTER V

The Rights of the Black Stole

Article I.—Funeral Fees

Canon 1234.—§1. Locorum Ordinarii indicem funeralium taxarum seu eleemosynarum, si non existat, pro suo territorio, de consilio Capituli cathedralis, ac, si opportunum duxerint, vicariorum foraneorum dioecesis et parochorum civitatis episcopalis, conficiant, attentis legitimis consuetudinibus particularibus et omnibus personarum et locorum circumstantiis; in eoque pro diversis casibus iura singulorum moderate determinent, ita ut quaelibet contentionum et scandali removeatur occasio.

§2. Si in indice plures classes enumerentur, liberum est iis quorum interest classem eligere.

Canon 1235.—§1. Districte prohibetur ne quis, sepulturae vel exsequiarum seu anniversarii mortuorum causa, quidquam exigat ultra id quod in dioecesano taxarum indice statuitur.

§2. Pauperes gratis omnino ac decenter funerentur et sepeliantur, cum exsequiis, secundum liturgicas leges et dioecesana statuta, praescriptis.

§1. *The Schedule of Fees.*—The law which governs the quantitative determination of stole fees in general expressly excepts funeral fees from the regulations it prescribes.[1] There is therefore no necessity to discuss this subject before the provincial council, since it is not required that a uniform schedule of fees obtain throughout the whole province; moreover, this schedule of fees does not need the approbation of the Holy See. If it does not already exist, the local Ordinary is obliged [2] to draw up a list of funeral

[1] Can. 1507, §1.

[2] *"Conficiant"*: Coronata, *De Loc. et Temp. Sacr.*, n. 245 and Rossi, *Sepult. Eccl. e l' Ius Fun.*, n. 92, interpret this as preceptive.

fees for his territory with the advice of the Cathedral Chapter, or, in our country, of the diocesan consultors.[3] Although he is not bound to follow this advice, it is necessary for validity that he at least consider what the consultors have to say, and if he acts without doing so his decree is without value and induces no obligation to abide by it.[4] If he considers it advisable, he should consult also the vicars forane, or rural deans, and the pastors of the episcopal city, but it is left to his own discretion to judge the utility of this. The wisdom of this counsel is evident, since both in determining the application and extension of the law and in estimating the various fees, legitimate customs and the varying circumstances of places and persons must be given due consideration; it is only reasonable, then, to suppose that those who are conversant with these facts are more competent than himself to speak of them.

The list of fees should, moreover, determine moderately and individually the rights of all concerned, so that all occasion of scandal and contention is removed.[5] If, as is permissible, different classes of funerals in conformity with liturgical requirements are enumerated, besides stating the amount for each kind of funeral service, the rights and portions of those who are entitled to share in it[6] and the amount of the stole fee should be severally defined. There may be also a different list of classes for the rural districts from that which obtains in the metropolitan area if this is considered expedient.[7]

---

[3] Can. 1234, §1.

[4] Can. 105, §1. Ojetti defends this view with arguments and authorities in *Ius Pontificium,* VII (1927), 13-25; Vermeersch-Creusen, *Epitome,* I, n. 197 bis, propounds the contrary opinion.

[5] Can. 1234, §1.

[6] ". . . nomine *taxae funeralis* non veniunt emolumenta dumtaxat quae ad parochum pertinent, verum etiam quae spectant ad alios presbyteros funus comitantes, ad aedituos aliosque altari inservientes, ad sodalitia, ad ceteros omnes qui partes agunt in funebri officio persolvendo . . .": Cappello, *De Visit. ad SS. Lim.,* Vol. II, cap. VII, tit. 70, sect. VIII, n. 3.

[7] Ferreres, *Le Confraternite,* t. II, n. 161 (quoted from Coronata, *De Loc. et Temp. Sacr.,* n. 245).

When more than one class of funeral service is indicated, the faithful are at liberty to choose the one they prefer.[8] From the fact that those who are concerned may not be restricted either directly or indirectly in electing a funeral service, it would seem that the practice of compelling the faithful to observe parochial offerings under threat of permitting only the lowest class is implicitly reprobated by this prescript.[9]

The canon which gives the Ordinary power to make this list of fees is in itself sufficient authority to permit him to change or revise it either in whole or in part, if fluctuation in the value of money or any other sufficient cause makes this expedient. But if this revision involves any substantial change in the existing law—and there is almost none which could be reasonably conceived as other than substantial—it is necessary that he again receive the advice of the Cathedral Chapter or of the diocesan consultors; otherwise his action is without legitimate effect.

It is left to the judgment of the Ordinary to determine the method of promulgating the Index of Funeral Fees. To publish them in the Diocesan Statutes, as is usually done, is sufficient to bring them to the attention of the clergy, but the faithful in general have an equal right to know the exact extent of their obligations in this respect. This knowledge might be brought to them either by inserting a notice in the official diocesan newspaper or in the parish magazines, or by posting a copy of the index in the Church sacristies. It would be less likely to give scandal to non-Catholics, however, if the pastors were directed to include it once a year in the announcements at the Masses on some Sunday or Holyday.

The legal sanction of the schedule of fees cannot be applied to or urged against those who can ill afford to abide

---

[8] Can. 1234, §2. This refers to the heirs, relatives, guardians, testamentary executors and so on. Cf. Rossi, *Sepult. Eccl. e l' Ius Funer.*, n. 92, N.B., footnote ad calc. p. 176.

[9] For the same reason, those who have been remiss in supporting the parish may not be constrained to accept a more expensive funeral service than they desire: Vermeersch-Creusen, *Epitome*, II, n. 540, 2.

by it.[10] Nevertheless, the poor are entitled to a decent funeral and burial both by the positive-divine law of Christian charity and by the common law of the Church; these services, moreover, are to be in strict accord with the prescriptions of liturgical laws and diocesan statutes,[11] and they must be provided absolutely without cost.[12] The obligation of providing these services devolves upon the proper pastor of the deceased, or, if the latter dies elsewhere and his corpse cannot be conveniently brought to his proper parish, upon the pastor of the place where death occurs. The reason for this is that pastors have not only the right, but the duty as well, to assist either personally or through a deputy at funeral services,[13] and it is only just that the one who would enjoy the right to the funeral fees should fulfill the duty of providing the services in the relatively small number of cases where these are not forthcoming.[14] The pastor, as was asserted above, is entitled to no remuneration for such services, unless by local custom the

[10] That is, when the estate of the deceased is insufficient to provide for his funeral and burial, or when his family, friends or others who would ordinarily be concerned to secure decent obsequies for his corpse are financially unable to do so.

[11] In defect of statute law on this point pastors should abide by local custom: Rossi, *Sepult. Eccl. e l' Ius Funer.*, n. 95.

[12] Can. 1235, §2; *Rit. Rom.*, tit. VI, cap. 1, n. 8. "Quod antiquissimi est instituti, illud, quantum fieri poterit, retineatur, ut Missa, praesente corpore defuncti, pro eo celebretur, antequam sepulturae tradatur": *ibid.*, n. 4. "Cum autem antiquissimi ritus ecclesiastici sit, cereos accensos in exsequiis et funeribus deferre, caveant item, ne eiusmodi ritus omittatur": *ibid.*, n. 7. "Per se ista obligatio etiam Missae celebrationem comprehendit quia id exsequiarum ordo, iuxta liturgicas leges includit; quare minus iuri communi conformia videntur statuta illarum dioeceseon aut consuetudines quae generatim parochos a Missae celebratione pro pauperibus omnino excusant; licet id admitti possit exceptionaliter . . .": Coronata, *De Loc. et Temp. Sacr.*, n. 245.

[13] Cf. Cans. 1230, §1, 1216 and 1218.

[14] For the same reason, namely, his duty towards the deceased, Rossi, *op. cit.*, n. 96, N.B. ad calc. p. 180, rightly declares that this obligation is incumbent upon the pastor even in the case where the heirs or parents of the deceased refuse to pay the funeral expenses though they are able to do so; he admits, however, that in this instance the obligation is not one of justice.

municipal authorities, a pious confraternity or some other agent assume responsibility for the expenses in these cases.[15] It is legitimate and wise, however, in the absence of such a praiseworthy custom, to formulate statute law on this question permitting the pastors, if they desire to do so, to charge the fees for the funerals of paupers to some more or less certain and sufficient source of parochial revenue. Thus the opportunity to practice pastoral charity would still be present for any pastor who desired to avail himself of it, and at the same time, where the burden of such funerals is distasteful or too onerous to the incumbent of the parochial office, the danger of scandal or contention would be safely removed.

With the one exception of paupers, who are legitimately and expressly exempted, the Index of Fees states the law for all concerned. For the laity it determines and decrees an obligation in justice, which the Ordinary [16] is authorized to enforce by virtue of canon 2349. It defines also the rights of the pastor and others engaged in the funeral service, and all are strictly forbidden to depart from the norm it establishes.[17] Pastors, therefore, may not under any pretext whatsoever demand more than that to which the index entitles them;[18] if they violate this point they are bound to restitution,[19] and this obligation cannot be otherwise interpreted than as one of justice. Their right to the tax itself, however, justifies them in demanding it within a reasonable

---

[15] Wernz, *Ius Decret.*, III, n. 786.

[16] N.B. Not the pastor himself.

[17] Even exempt religious must conform to its prescriptions. Pont. Commis., 6 Mar. 1927—*AAS*, XIX (1927), 161: "Jam vero privilegium exemptionis non afficit nisi personas, domus, ecclesias regularium . . . cum, vel in ecclesia aut intra monasterii septa populus admittitur, vel regulares extra exemptum territorium prodeunt, tum seu ratione territorii seu ratione populi, Ordinarii loci auctoritati exclusive subiecti, subintrat potestas eiusdem Ordinarii . . .". "Salvo tamen iure immemorabilis coram Iudice probandae"; ita Pallotini, *Collect. Resolut. S. C. C.*, XIV, v. *Parochus*, §VII, n. 24.

[18] Can. 1235, §1; Pallotini, *op. cit.*, XIV, v. *Parochus*, §VII, n. 23; Vecchiotti, *Inst. Canon.*, lib. III, cap. V. §60; S. C. C., in *Senogallien.*, 11 Apr. 1739—*Thesaur. Resolut. S. C. C.*, IX, 36-37.

[19] Can. 463, §2.

time after the funeral ceremonies if it is not voluntarily offered and, as all commentators are agreed, is basis for juridical action against those who can meet this obligation yet refuse to do so; the funeral or burial, however, may in no way be impeded or delayed to compel them to offer the taxes beforehand.[20]

§2. *The Right to Funeral Fees.* As with Baptism, Marriage, and other functions, the administration of which is indicative of jurisdiction in the external forum, so too, the collation of Christian burial is a strictly parochial function, reserved by common law to the proper pastor of the deceased.[21] The funeral service is, as it were, the complement of the sacraments, so that the right to assist at the former is ordinarily dependent upon the right to administer the sacraments.[22] The pastor's right to the funeral offerings of his parishioners, which is in turn a consequence of his right to assist at their funerals, is two-fold: whenever they are buried from their proper parish he is entitled to a certain determined offering; and when they are buried from another parish, he is entitled to receive the parochial portion,[23] unless the pastor of the church of burial is excused from refunding this part of the fees for the legitimate causes mentioned below.[24]

The proper pastor and parish of the deceased are determined by domicile and quasi-domicile.[25] The question as to whether or not the parish of quasi-domicile can be considered the proper parish for funerals has frequently been decided in the affirmative by the Congregation of the Coun-

[20] Cf. Wernz, *Ius Decret.*, III, n. 786; Rossi, *Sepult. Eccl. e l' Ius Funer.*, n. 93; Smith, *Counterpoints in Canon Law*, nn. 188 ss.

[21] Cans. 462, 5° and 1230, §1.

[22] Barbosa, *De Offic. et Pot. Paroch.*, Pars III, cap. XXVI, n. 34.

[23] S. C. C., in *Romana et Bredanen.* 27 Aug. 1904—*ASS*, XXXVII, 464; Bouix, *De Parocho*, Pars IV, cap. X, III; Capello, *De Visit. SS. Limin*, vol. II, cap. VII, tit. 70, sect. VIII, n. 1.

[24] The destination of the fees when another takes the place of the pastor, either as his delegate or with his permission, has been sufficiently explained in the commentary on canon 463, §3. See Ch. III, art. I, §§6 & 7.

[25] Can. 94, §1; S. C. C., in *Romana et Bredanen.*, 27 Aug. 1904, *supra cit.*

cil.[26] Diocesan statute or legitimate custom, however, may restrict the meaning of proper parish so as to indicate only the parish of domicile.[27] With this exception, however, the general rule obtains that the pastor of quasi-domicile is equally competent to assist with the pastor of domicile; nor does the method of acquiring domicile or quasi-domicile affect this right: whether they are acquired by protracted residence, or merely by assuming residence with the intention to remain, either fact is juridically sufficient to endow the pastor with the right to perform the funeral functions. To the contention that it is practically equivalent to defrauding the former pastor of the funeral fees when death occurs within a relatively short time after a change of residence, the Congregation of the Council has justified the principle underlying this law by asserting that what a pastor loses one day he gains another, when the circumstances which are against him are in his favor.[28]

Unhappily, the Code nowhere in the tract on Ecclesiastical Sepulture explicitly indicates the pastor to whom the funeral fees are due, except in canon 1236 where directions are given for refunding the parochial portion. It confines itself for the most part to determining the proper church for funerals, so that it is necessary to revert to the principle that offerings made on the occasion of parochial functions licitly performed, belong to the pastor of the church in which they are administered, to reach a conclusion that is admitted by all, though not expressly contained in the

[26] In *Melevitana*, 2 June 1917—*AAS*, X (1918), 328; Response to Card. Logue, Archbp. Armagh, 14 June 1923: "An post Codicem I. C. paroecia etiam quasi domicilii sit paroecia propria defuncti ad effectum percipiendi emolumenta funeraria in casu." Resp.: "Affirmative." — *Irish Eccl. Record*, XXII (1923), 194.

[27] Many, *De Locis Sacris*, n. 172, 2°, b). The time required for such a custom to prescribe the right of the pastor of quasi-domicile is controverted: ita S. C. C., in *Melevitana*, 2 June 1917—*AAS*, X (1918), 329, which does not decide the question. "Legitimae consuetudines necnon statuta particularia multum operantur in materia funerum, adeo ut vel ipsi iuri communi aliquando derogent." — S. C. EE. et RR., in *Pisauren*, 5 May 1905—*ASS*, XXXVIII, 207.

[28] In *Melevitana*, 2 June 1917—*AAS*, X (1918), 330; in *Ardachaden.*, 9 June 1923—*AAS*, XVIII (1926), 509.

Code, namely: that the pastor of the church to which the right to hold the funeral is assigned is entitled to receive the funeral fees. He may not always retain them all, but must sometimes return the parochial portion, or otherwise apportion them as the Index of Funeral Fees directs him.[29]

Unless the deceased has chosen another church for his funeral, his proper pastor has the right to bury him and to retain the funeral fees whenever his death occurs in his own parish or in a place from which it is convenient to bring the body by a journey on foot to his proper parish.[30] If the deceased has more than one proper parish by reason of domicile or quasi-domicile, the right to assist at his funeral and to receive the funeral fees is vested in the pastor of the parish within whose limits he dies;[31] nor is the latter under any obligation to restore the parochial portion to the other proper pastor or pastors of the deceased. But when the deceased dies elsewhere than in one of his proper parishes, the pastor of the nearest proper parish, if he can conveniently be brought there, enjoys the same rights as though death had occurred in his parish.[32]

The local Ordinary is to determine for his own territory the distance and other circumstances [33] which render the transfer of the corpse from the place of death to the church of the funeral service or the place of burial inconvenient, having first considered the peculiarities of climate, topography and so on appropriate to the place.[34] When the

[29] This conclusion must be borne in mind in investigating many of the references that follow, since very often the only authority for asserting that this or that pastor is entitled to the fees is a canon directing that the funeral be held in his church. Cf. Coronata, *De Loc. et Temp. Sacr.*, n. 246.

[30] Cans. 1216, §1 and 1218, §1.

[31] Can. 1216, §2.

[32] Can. 1218, §1.

[33] For example, the season of the year if this affects the possibility of travel.

[34] Can. 1218, §2. If expedient, this designation of inconvenience may vary for different sections of the same territory: Blat, *Commentarium*, III, n. 76. Although it is not required by the Code, there would seem to be the same reasons for having the advice of the diocesan consultors in defining this point as in determining the Index of Fees.

place of death and the church of funeral pertain to different dioceses, inconvenience according as it is determined by the Ordinary of the diocese where death occurs is to be regarded.[35] Even though the distance exceeds that which is determined as inconvenient, if the family, heirs, relatives of the deceased or others concerned are willing to bear the expenses of transportation, the corpse is to be brought to the proper church and pastor of the deceased, or, if he had more than one, to the nearest.[36]

When death occurs in a parish where the deceased has neither domicile nor quasi-domicile, if it is inconvenient to transfer the body to its proper parish and those concerned are unwilling to incur the expenses of having this done, the pastor of the place of death is entitled to hold the funeral services and to retain the fees.[37] The pastor of the place of death enjoys these same rights whenever the deceased has nowhere a proper pastor and parish by reason of parochial domicile or quasi-domicile.[38] The same is true of the pastor of the church of elective funeral, as often as the distance from the scene of death to what is the deceased's proper parish exceeds that which is defined as inconvenient for transfer.[39] It is to be remembered, however, that whenever the right of a church other than the parochial church of the deceased is doubtful, the right of the parochial church—that is, the right of the deceased's proper pastor to perform the functions and to receive the emoluments—should always prevail.[40]

The above paragraphs enumerate practically all the instances that commonly occur wherein the pastor who performs the funeral services is entitled to receive and to retain the fees with no obligation to return the parochial

---

[35] Can. 1218, §2.

[36] Can. 1218, §3.

[37] Can. 1218, §1.

[38] Cans. 94, §2 and 1230, §1.

[39] Can. 1236, §1.

[40] Can. 1217.

portion to another pastor.[41] Attention is given in the succeeding pages to the parochial portion and to the cases that involve its return to the proper pastor or pastors of the deceased.

Article II.—The Parochial Portion

Canon 1236.—§1. Salvo iure particulari, quoties fidelis non funeratur in ecclesia paroeciali propria, proprio defuncti parocho debetur portio paroecialis, excepto casu quo cadaver in ecclesiam propriae paroeciae commode asportari nequeat.

§2. Si quis habeat plures paroecias proprias ad quas cadaver commode deferri posset, et alibi funeretur, portio paroecialis dividenda est inter omnes parochos proprios.

Canon 1237.—§1. Detrahi debet portio paroecialis ex omnibus et solis emolumentis, quae statuta sunt pro funere et tumulatione in taxa dioecesana.

§2. Si quacunque de causa primum sollemne officium funebre non statim, sed intra mensem completum a die tumulationis fiat, licet hoc die non defuerint minora publica officia, portio tamen paroecialis ex huius etiam funeris emolumentis debetur.

§3. Quantitas portionis paroecialis determinetur in taxa dioecesana; et si ecclesia paroecialis et ecclesia funerans ad diversas dioeceses pertineant, quantitas portionis paroecialis attenditur secundum taxam ecclesiae funerantis.

Because of his constant vigilance for the spiritual welfare of his parishioners, the pastor has the right to assist at their funerals and burial and to receive the offerings made on these occasions. Observing the traditional respect and reverence for the wishes of the dead, however, the Code, in conformity with previous legislation, admits the juridical effect of elective sepulture, by which all who are not ex-

[41] Fees for the funerals of religious, seminarians and others whose domicile is of an institutional nature are treated in Chapter VI. Those for the funerals of the Pope, of Cardinals, Bishops and other prelates, of beneficiaries and so on are omitted, since they are of relatively rare occurrence and more limited interest; they belong properly to more comprehensive studies; cf. Rossi, Coronata, Many, *et al.*

pressly forbidden by law are permitted to choose the church of their funeral or the cemetery of their burial.[42] In conciliating these two fundamental ideas of ecclesiastical sepulture, the Church declares that, unless particular law ordains otherwise[43] or transfer of the body to the proper parish is inconvenient, as often as the funeral is held in a church other than the proper parochial church, the parochial portion of the funeral fees is due to the proper pastor of the deceased; and in the same hypotheses, if the latter had more than one proper parish to which his body might conveniently be brought, the parochial portion is to be divided between or among all these pastors.[44]

The parochial portion may be defined as that part of the funeral offerings accruing to the church of funeral which the latter[45] must cede to the proper pastor of the deceased.[46] The quantity of the parochial portion according

---

[42] Cans. 1223 and 1226. Title to ancestral or hereditary sepulchre is practically equivalent to elective sepulture (cf. can. 1229); but if, having such a sepulchre in one place (not his proper parish), the deceased elects to be buried elsewhere, or if his corpse cannot be brought conveniently to the ancestral sepulchre from the place of death, the pastor of the parish where he possesses ancestral sepulchre has no title to share in the fees, since he is not the proper pastor of the deceased, and because the parochial portion was instituted only in favor of the proper pastor: Coronata, *De Loc. et Temp. Sacr.*, n. 248, e); Many, *De Locis Sacr.*, n. 202, 7°.

[43] Particular law may sanction the practice of not solving the parochial portion: Coronata, *op. cit.*, n. 248, a); so, too, may legitimate custom. "By custom or prescription the obligation of paying the quarta funeralis has been done away with in most places, . . .": Dunford, "Funeral Dues," *Cath. Encycl.*, VI, 321.

[44] Can. 1236, §§1 and 2.

[45] To recover this, there is no basis for action against the heirs, relatives or friends of the deceased. "Pro exactione quartae funeralis non gravatur haeres, sed lis agitur inter Parochum et Ecclesiam tumulantem." — S. C. EE. et RR., 14 July 1865 (quoted by Rossi, *Sepult. Eccl. e l' Ius Funer.*, n. 100, 2)).

[46] Many, *De Locis Sacris*, n. 201, 1°; Coronata, *De Loc. et Temp. Sacr.*, n. 247; Cappello, *De Visit. SS. Limin.*, vol. II, cap. VII, tit. 70, sect. VIII, n. 5.

to common law is one-fourth,[47] but by local custom it may be also one-third or one-half the funeral offerings.[48] The Bishop is to state in the Index of Fees the quantity of the parochial portion;[49] he must therefore observe the prescriptions given in canon 1234, §1, for determining other items of the Index of Funeral Fees.[50] Whenever the church of funeral pertains to a diocese different from that of the proper parish of the deceased, the quantity of the parochial portion is to be that which is stated in the Index of Fees for the diocese of the church of funeral.[51]

The parochial portion should consist of a part of all the fees [52] assigned for funeral and burial in the diocesan taxes, and of them alone.[53] In stating the amount of the parochial portion the Ordinary may either declare that a certain fraction of the various fees must be returned to the proper pastor, or he may determine this amount quantitatively for the various classes listed in the Index.[54] From common law there is no authority for deducting this portion from bequests for Masses for the deceased, from the fees for the

[47] C. 8, X, *de sepult.*, III, 28; Reiffenstuel, *Ius Canon. Univers.*, lib. III, tit. XXVIII, n. 48; Vecchiotti, *Inst. Canon.* lib. III, cap. V, §61; Many, *op. cit.*, n. 205, 2°; Cappello, *l. c.* Whence it is also termed the "*quarta canonica*" or "*quarta funeralis.*"

[48] C. 9, X, *de sepult.*, III, 28. For obvious reasons it should not exceed one-half: Coronata, *op. cit.*, n. 251, c).

[49] Can. 1237, §3. In determining this, local customs must be given due consideration: cf. S. C. C., in *Camerien*, 18 Dec. 1819, ad II^{um}—*Thesaur. Resolut. S. C. C.*, LXXIX, 342; Many, *op. cit.*, n. 205, 1°; Cappello, *l. c.* The Index of Fees should, moreover, take into account acquired rights and exemptions granted to certain parishes or communities, which legitimately release them from the obligation of refunding the parochial portion or of observing other prescriptions of general or particular law: Coronata, *De Loc. et Temp. Sacr.*, n. 245.

[50] Coronata, *l. c.* n. 251, a).

[51] Can. 1237, §3.

[52] Except the Mass stipend, which should remain integral: Cocchi, *Commentarium*, lib. III, n. 68; Vito, *Quistioni Canoniche*, I, n. 4, footnote 2 ad calc. p. 18; Vermeersch-Creusen, *Epitome*, II, n. 544, 1.

[53] Can. 1237, §1.

[54] For example, five dollars for the first class, four for the second, and so on: Rossi, *Sepult. Eccl. e l' Ius Funer.*, n. 97, nota ad calc. pp. 183-184; Coronata, *De Loc. et Temp. Sacr.*, n. 251, b).

exequial service of the third, seventh, or thirtieth day or the anniversary of death;[55] but just as local custom can determine the quantity of the parochial portion, so, too, it may legitimately decree the sources from which it is to be subtracted.[56] If for any reason the first solemn funeral office is not held immediately but occurs within one complete month from the day of burial,[57] the parochial portion must be deducted both from the fees for this service and from those for any less solemn office that may have taken place on the day of burial.[58]

A few principles evident from canons 1236 and 1237 are sufficient to solve the ordinary cases involving the parochial portion. These are: that the proper pastor never pays the parochial portion; that none but the proper pastor is entitled to receive it; and that only cases of elective funeral or ancestral sepulture necessitate it, and these only when death occurs either in one's proper parish or in a place from which transportation of the body to its proper parish is convenient.

Since the pastor of the place of death is the proper pastor for the funeral of one who has nowhere a parochial domi-

---

[55] Rossi, *op. cit.*, n. 99; Coronata, *op. cit.*, n. 250; Blat, *op. cit.*, lib. III, n. 97; Vermeersch-Creusen, *op. cit.*, II, n. 544; Many, *De Locis Sacris*, n. 204, 3°.

[56] Reiffenstuel, *Ius Canon. Univers.*, lib. III, tit. XXVIII, n. 52; Many, *op. cit.*, n. 204, 4°.

[57] To be computed according to the calendar beginning with the midnight immediately following burial: can. 34, §3, 1° & 3°. If, for a legitimate reason, the solemn service cannot be held within this month but occurs later, the canonical portion will not be due according to common law: Vermeersch-Creusen, *Epitome*, II, n, 544, 2. When asked whether a funeral office held within one month from the time news of the death arrived from a distant country, or one purposely delayed beyond the month to defraud the proper pastor of the portion, might be considered the solemn first office of canon 1237, §2, the Commission for the Interpretation of the Code declared that recourse must be had to the Sacred Congregation of the Council: 24 Nov. 1920—*AAS*, XII (1920), 573.

[58] Can. 1237, §2. It would seem that the "first solemn funeral office" refers to the funeral Mass: Coronata, *De Loc. et Temp. Sacr.*, n. 250; Vermeersch-Creusen, *Epitome*, II, n. 544, 2; Blat, *Commentarium*, lib. III, n. 97.

cile or quasi-domicile, it follows that he is entitled to the parochial portion if the latter is legitimately buried from another church. If, having more than one proper parish, one dies and is buried elsewhere, the portion is to be divided among all and only those of his proper pastors to whose parishes the body could be conveniently transferred; and if the deceased in this instance dies in one of his proper parishes and is buried elsewhere, the pastor of the proper parish in which death occurs is alone entitled to receive the portion, since he alone is competent to assist at the funeral according to canon 1216.[59]

It is to be remembered that whatever is said of funerals above refers only to the first solemn funeral office. If, on the occasion of transfer of the cadaver to another cemetery or for any other reason, the funeral services are repeated,[60] no pastor enjoys competence to assist to the exclusion of others, whether or not the first funeral took place in the proper parish, provided only that the first funeral was in accordance with the law; the family, friends or those responsible are in this case at liberty to choose any pastor they prefer to perform the ceremonies, and he is entitled to retain the fees, even though he is not the proper pastor of the deceased; nor is there any obligation of returning the parochial portion to the latter.[61]

The legal presumption that election of sepulture or title to ancestral burial includes election of the church to which the cemetery pertains for the funeral service has no foundation in common law; it is based on the much quoted phrase *"ubi tumulus ibi funus,"* and is recognized only in those territories where custom or statute sanctions it, as, for example, in Italy.[62] Elsewhere the election of sepulture in a particular cemetery implies that and nothing more.

---

[59] Cf. Coronata, *De Loc. et Temp. Sacr.*, n. 248.

[60] It is permitted, but not of obligation to repeat them.

[61] S. C. C., in *Sanct. Severin.*, 12 Jan. 1924—*AAS*, XVI (1924), 190-191; in *Barcinon.*, 27 Aug. 1904—*ASS*, XXXVII, 537.

[62] Vermeersch, "Ubi tumulus ibi funus," *Periodica*, XVI (1927), 57*—66*. Others declare that this presumption is based on common law, and would apply it universally: Many, *De Locis Sacris*, nn. 189-190; Coronata, *De Loc. et Temp. Sacr.*, n. 187.

There would seem to be nothing in the tract on Ecclesiastical Sepulture to justify the universal application of the above axiom. On the contrary, the syntactical interpretation of the particle *"aut"* in canons 1223, 1224 and 1226, which discuss the right and valor of election, is directly opposed to this; and since the question is one which involves parochial rights, it admits only a strict interpretation.

Where the funeral service occurs in the church of one parish and burial in the cemetery of another (not the proper parish), the pastor of the place of burial has no title to the parochial portion, since this is exclusively the right of the proper pastor.

If the corpse is sent to a place where the deceased had neither his proper parish nor a legitimately elected church of funeral, the right to the funeral and burial belongs to the cathedral church or, for lack of such, to the parochial church within whose limits the cemetery is located, unless custom or diocesan statute ordains otherwise.[63] Coronata,[64] implicitly applying the principle *"ubi tumulus ibi funus,"* uses this injunction to determine the church of funeral when title to ancestral sepulture pertains to a common cemetery. Since, as was asserted above, that principle is not recognized everywhere, this interpretation of canon 1230, §7 can be applied, if at all, only where the axiom favoring it is accepted. It would seem, rather, that this prescription, as Vermeersch [65] states, was intended to cover only rare and extraordinary cases in which solution from other sources is impossible, as, for example, when death occurs on a train,[66] or on shipboard not followed by burial at sea. In such cases, the rector of the Cathedral, or the pastor of the parish in whose territory the cemetery is situated, is entitled to assist at the funeral and to retain the fees, presupposing, of course, the lack of elective funeral, and the inconvenience of transporting the body to its proper parish.

---

[63] Can. 1230, §7.

[64] *De Loc. et Temp. Sacr.*, nn. 187 & 204.

[65] *Periodica,* XVI (1927), 67*—70*.

[66] Rossi, *Sepult. Eccl. e l' Ius Funer.*, n. 55, 8.

When the church chosen for the funeral is not exempt from the jurisdiction of the pastor and the deceased was a parishioner of the latter, the pastor has the right to assist at the funeral services,[67] but he is entitled to receive only the parochial portion, not the entire funeral offerings,[68] since this is not the proper parish church of the deceased.

Exemption from the obligation of paying the parochial portion must be based on privilege, custom or prescription.[69] By custom, as was asserted above, it can be, and in some localities has been entirely abolished; and the same is true of legitimate prescription. The Roman Pontiffs have frequently granted to Orders and Monasteries exemption from the payment of the parochial portion. Those not revoked by the Council of Trent,[70] those conceded after that Council, and, for Italy and its adjacent islands, those granted after the general annulment of all privileges by Benedict XIII,[71] are still in force.

---

67 Can. 1230, §4 "*salvo peculiari privilegio.*"

68 Many, *De Locis Sacris*, n. 200, 4°; Coronata, *De Loc. et Temp. Sacr.*, n. 217, b). Vecchiotti, *Instit. Canon.*, lib. III, cap. V, §60, makes the following distinction: if such a church has no proper rector, the pastor of the parish where it is situated has all the rights; if it has a proper rector, he receives the funeral offerings and gives the parochial portion to the pastor.

69 Cf. Many, *De Locis Sacris*, n. 203.

70 Sess. XXV, *de Ref.*, cap. 13.

71 Const. "*Romanus Pontifex,*" 28 April 1725, praesert. §§3 & 4—*Fontes*, I, n. 284.

CHAPTER VI

Exemption

Exemption in general is the right by which a physical or moral person or a place is withdrawn from the ordinary jurisdiction and power to which it is subject by common law.[1] This exemption is twofold, namely, either as regards temporal administration, or with reference to spiritual care; the former releases the subject of the exemption from the jurisdiction of the Ordinary; the latter—and this is the species of exemption that is in question here—not only withdraws the institution from the care of the pastor within whose territory it is situated,[2] but in some instances also suspends the effect of the various forms of canonical residence upon the licit administration of parochial functions, so that consequently a lack of such residence in an exempt institution often has no influence on the right to stole fees.

Strictly speaking, common law assigns to the pastor the right to perform all parochial functions within his parish limits; by way of exception, however, this same authority exempts certain communities and places from his care, as in canons 514 and 1368. Moreover, the privilege of exemption may also be acquired either through pontifical or episcopal concession or through custom.[3] This exemp-

[1] S. R. Rota, in *Vincentina,* 29 Mar. 1915, n. 4—*AAS,* VII (1915), 335.

[2] *Ibid.,* n. 5.

[3] S. C. C., in *Lisbonen.,* 21 April 1917—*AAS,* X (1918), 141-142; S. R. Rota, in *Bergomen.,* 25 Feb. 1919—*AAS,* XII (1920), 131; Many, *De Locis Sacris,* n. 172, 5°, b). The controversy as to whether or not a Bishop could confer this exemption—pro: Wernz, *Ius Decretal.,* II, n. 878; contra: De Luca, *De Parochis,* Disc. XXIII, nn. 11 & 12—is settled in the affirmative by canon 464, §2.

tion may be either complete and absolute or partial, so that it may assign the right to perform all or only certain parochial functions; its extension must be determined either from the law or document conceding it, or, if the exemption is acquired through custom, it must be strictly interpreted to cover only those functions which have been legitimately prescribed.[4] In no case may the exemption be extended beyond what it actually concedes, and in any controversy, either regarding the exemption itself or its application, the burden of proof lies with those who claim the exemption.[5] It is to be noted, finally,—and this applies whether or not it is exempt—that an institution is never considered neutral territory; so that there is no justification for anyone not responsible for the care of those residing in such an institution to assist at a parochial function there, even though the subject be his parishioner, without the permission of the one entitled to exercise that care.

The rights of a pastor within whose parish limits a non-exempt institution is located are practically equivalent to those which the chaplain of an exempt institution ordinarily enjoys. When these rights are not defined by documents or otherwise determined, they must be understood to extend only to what the nature of the institution demands. If it is one wherein the inmates ordinarily acquire domicile or quasi-domicile, the one in whom the spiritual care is vested is undoubtedly competent to perform all parochial functions and entitled to retain the fees offered on such occasions; but where this hypothesis is not verified—and this is most often true of hospitals—the rights of the pastors of those who are temporarily resident in such institutions cannot lightly be disregarded. The common law of the Church demands that the relation of domicile, quasi-domicile, or, for marriage, monthly residence, must ordinarily exist between the minister and the subject of a parochial function. Because of the necessity of the faithful and the inconvenience of securing their proper pastors, the one in charge

[4] Cf. S. R. Rota, in *Vincentina*, 29 Mar. 1915, n. 10—*AAS*, VII (1915), 337.

[5] *Ibid.*, n. 6—*AAS*, VII (1915), 336.

of the spiritual care of a hospital[6] can licitly administer the sacraments of Penance, Eucharist or Viaticum and Extreme Unction, even though the last three are usually reserved to the proper pastor.[7] The nature of such an institution, however, is ordinarily insufficient to justify the administration of the sacraments of Baptism and Matrimony,[8] or the celebration of funeral services.[9]

The licit collation of solemn Baptism ordinarily requires not only a proper minister but also a proper place. The minister is he who has jurisdiction over the one to be baptized by reason of the latter's domicile or quasi-domicile; the place is the baptistry of a church or public oratory.[10] Where these two facts are verified, the one to whom the spiritual care of those dwelling in an institution has been confided may assist licitly and retain the fee.

This question arises most frequently, however, with regard to hospitals, and here almost invariably either one or both the above requisites is absent. Only rarely is a hospital the proper place for solemn Baptism, since hospital chapels ordinarily must be considered semi-public oratories.[11] The fact of exemption is certainly insufficient to excuse the chaplain from observing the demands of the Ritual and of common law that solemn baptism be administered in a church or a public oratory; moreover, there is express prohibition against celebrating ecclesiastical functions in a semi-public oratory whenever this would be contrary to rubrical requirements.[12] Nor is there any basis for the "*a fortiori*" argument that, if for a grave and reasonable cause the Ordinary may permit the collation of solemn baptism in a private home in some extraordinary

---

[6] The chaplain, if it is exempt from the pastor's jurisdiction; otherwise the latter.

[7] Cf. cans. 462, 2° & 3°, 848, §1 and 938, §2.

[8] S. R. Rota, in *Vincentina*, 29 Mar. 1915, n. 4—*AAS*, VII (1915), 335.

[9] Cf. canon 1222.

[10] Cans. 462, 1°, 94, §1 and 773; *Rit. Rom.*, tit. II, cap. I, n. 42.

[11] S. C. Rit., *Decr. super Orat. Semi-pub.*, 23 Jan. 1899—*ASS*, XXXI, 412.

[12] Can. 1193.

case,[13] he may also permit it as a practice in a semi-public oratory, or, much less, in a non-Catholic hospital or one without a chapel.

If, then, the hospital chapel is not a public oratory, the question arises, when may such baptisms be conferred licitly in the church of the parish within whose limits the hospital is situated, or, in other words, when may the relation of domicile or quasi-domicile which must ordinarily exist between subject and minister be disregarded. Whether or not the hospital is exempt, the pastor of the territory where it is located is alone competent to assist at solemn baptism in the parochial church or any place not exempt from his jurisdiction. But he is not the proper pastor of all infants born in such a hospital, only of those whose fathers [14] have either domicile or quasi-domicile in his parish, or have none at all; for the rest, the same holds true, the pastor of the father's [14] domicile or quasi-domicile is the proper pastor for the baptism of the child.[15] If the latter can be brought to its proper pastor conveniently and without delay, he alone is entitled to baptize; otherwise the pastor of the parish where the hospital is located may confer solemn baptism and consequently retain the fee.[16] The two circumstances of inconvenience and delay have been sufficiently explained in the commentary on Baptism.[17] They must be verified simultaneously, and if the infant can be taken to its proper parish church either while the mother is still in the hospital, or within a reasonable time after mother and child have returned to their home, no other pastor is justified in conferring solemn baptism. Authors vary so widely in estimating what length of time constitutes a grave delay that it is useless to try to reconcile their views.[18] Provided the parents have a serious intention of not neglecting baptism,

---

[13] Can. 776, §1, 2°.

[14] Or mothers, for illegitimate and posthumous children: can. 90, §1.

[15] Cans. 90, §§1 & 2 and 738.

[16] Can. 738, §2.

[17] See ch. IV, art. I.

[18] Cf. S. Alphons. de Liguor., *Theol. Moral.*, lib. VI, n. 118.

delay cannot be considered grave unless there is reason to fear the danger of death, or unless it exceeds what particular law defines as grave delay.[19] Ten days after childbirth is the time mothers usually leave a hospital, so that according to sound authors [20] they have from two to three weeks after that time to secure baptism for their children without being guilty of grave delay.

Assistance at marriage in institutions offers less difficulty than Baptism. The requirements as to the proper place are not so stringent as with the latter sacrament. The Ordinary is empowered to permit the celebration of matrimony either in public or semi-public oratories;[21] and the mere fact of exemption, if it includes permission to assist at marriage, may be considered to contain implicit permission to hold the function in such places.[22] For licit assistance, however, and that the minister may be entitled to retain the fee, it is necessary that at least one of the parties to the contract have a domicile, quasi-domicile or a month's residence in the institution,[23] unless the minister derives his competence from the grave necessity mentioned in canon 1097, §1, 3°.

For hospitals, exempt or non-exempt, the case of necessity is ordinarily the only one which justifies the celebration of this sacrament, even though the inmates of such institutions frequently fulfill the canonical requirements of a month's residence. The reason for this is that hospital exemption refers primarily and ordinarily to the adminis-

---

19 Genicot, *Theologia Moralis*, II, n. 146; Ballerini, *Opus Theol. Moral.*, Tract. X, sect. II, n. 40.

20 Vermeersch-Creusen, *Epitome*, II, n. 52; Cappello, *De Sacramentis*, I, n. 149, 1°.

21 Can. 1109, §1; the pastor of the parish where a non-exempt house is situated may do likewise. This presupposes, of course, that both parties are Catholics.

22 Cf. *Amer. Eccl. Rev.*, LXXVII (1927), 93-95. In the churches and oratories of Seminaries and religious women, however, this sacrament may not be celebrated, except in an extraordinary case with the permission of the Ordinary: can. 1109, §2.

23 What was asserted in the commentary on Marriage Fees of the requirements for contracting these various residences applies here; see ch. IV, art. II, §1.

tration of the sacraments which are necessary for those confined in such institutions, namely, Penance, Eucharist or Viaticum and Extreme Unction, and cannot, as a rule, be extended to the celebration of marriage,[24] unless in a particular case it is certain from the document conceding the exemption that this is permitted.[25]

The Rector of a Seminary is entitled to conduct the funeral of all who live within the territory of the institution, and to receive the fees for this function; and if another church has been chosen for the ceremonies he can claim the parochial portion.[26] The Superior of clerical religious[27] has the same rights to hold the funeral and to receive the fees for the exequies of those under his charge—religious, novices,[28] and servants living night and day within the territory of the institution—provided that death occurs in the institution or in a place from which it is convenient according to canon 1218, §3 to transfer the body to it; where it is inconvenient to do this the pastor of the place of death has these rights.[29] When novices or the servants who live night and day within the exempt territory elect to have their funerals elsewhere, the religious Superior is entitled to the parochial portion.

---

[24] S. R. Rota, in *Vincentina*, 29 Mar. 1915, n. 10—*AAS*, VII (1915), 337; De Luca, *De Parochis*, Disc. XXIII, n. 19; Disc. XXXVIII, nn. 9-12; Disc. XLI, n. 3. These authorities assert the same for Baptism.

[25] S. R. Rota, in *Vincentina*, 29 Mar. 1915, *l. c.*; Santi. *Praelect. Jur. Canon.*, lib. I, tit. XXXIII, n. 2. Canon 1368, which grants to Seminaries exemption from the jurisdiction of the local pastor, expressly excepts Matrimony from this exemption.

[26] Cans. 1222, 1368 and 1236, §1.

[27] For laical male religious and exempt women religious, the chaplain, and for non-exempt women religious, the pastor of the parish where their house is situated, have the same rights as the Superior of clerical religious: Cf. Coronata, *De Loc. et Temp. Sacr.*, n. 212, 3° & 4°.

[28] This does not includes postulants: Pont. Comiss., 29 Jul. 1929, ad IV—*AAS*, XXI (1929), 573.

[29] Cans. 1221 and 1230, §5. If such servants die outside the institution and have one or more other canonical residences, the proper parish for the funeral is determined by canons 1216-1218.

For those who die in hospitals, colleges and other institutions,[30] if they have acquired domicile or quasi-domicile there, or if they have none elsewhere or cannot be conveniently transported to their proper parish, the chaplain or the pastor of the parish in which the institution is located, according as it is exempt or not, is competent to perform the funeral services and entitled to retain the fees, since the funerals of such persons are governed by the general prescripts of canons 1216–1218.[31]

The insane have the domicile of their curators or guardians.[32] There is no basis for controversy when the chaplain of an asylum where they are confined, or the pastor of the parish where it is situated, if the institution is not exempt from his care, is entitled by particular law or privilege to conduct their funerals;[33] otherwise their right to assist at this function and to receive the fees for it depends upon the interpretation of the word "*curatoris*" of canon 93. Maroto [34] contends that they retain the domicile of their natural or legal guardians, and, in defect of such, that they preserve their last domicile before entering such institutions.[35] To interpret it to mean the domicile of their *actual* curator, so that they acquire domicile in the asylum through the intention of their natural or legal guardians,[36] would seem to be equally legitimate and more in consonance with

---

[30] The houses of Regulars also, if they dwell there as guests, students or invalids.

[31] Can. 1222.

[32] Can. 93, §1.

[33] Can. 1222; S. R. Rota, in *Bergomen.*, 25 Feb. 1919—*AAS*, XII (1920), 131, 133-134.

[34] *Apollinaris*, I (1928), 506-510.

[35] He bases these opinions on the premises that they are incapable of having the intention of acquiring a domicile in the asylum, and that they are not presumed to have the intention of leaving their previous domicile, since they are equally incapable of this. Kinane says that ". . . if he has not a guardian, he is necessarily without either domicile or quasi-domicile, and must be put in the category of vagi": *Irish Eccl. Record*, XXVI (1925), 637.

[36] Cf. S. C. C., in *Pisauren.*, 14 May 1887—*Thesaur. Resolut. S. C. C.*, CXLVI, 223-224; in *Pisauren.*, 27 Jan. 1917—*AAS*, IX (1917), 272-273.

the theory that the church which ordinarily has the right of funeral is that in which the deceased was accustomed to attend divine services and to receive the sacraments,[37] and consequently that the one who is entitled to the funeral offerings is the one who cared for the spiritual needs of the defunct, that is, the pastor of the asylum, or, if it is exempt, the chaplain.

[37] C. 2, *de sepult.*, III, 12 in VI°.

UNIVERSITAS CATHOLICA AMERICAE

WASHINGTON, D. C.

FACULTAS IURIS CANONICI

1930

No. 59

DEUS LUX MEA

TITULI

QUOS

AD DOCTORATUS GRADUM

IN

JURE CANONICO

APUD UNIVERSITATEM CATHOLICAM AMERICAE

CONSEQUENDUM

PUBLICE PROPUGNABIT

GULIELMUS A. FERRY

SACERDOS DIOECESIS PHILADELPHIENSIS

JURIS CANONICI LICENTIATUS

HORA XI AM DIE XXVI MAII MCMXXX

TITULI

DE JURE CANONICO

I.	De Dissertatione.	
II.	De Historia Juris Canonici.	
III.	Canones 1-7	De Ambitu Codicis.
IV.	Canones 8-24	De Legibus Ecclesiasticis.
V.	Canones 25-30	De Consuetudine.
VI.	Canones 31-35	De Temporis Supputatione.
VII.	Canones 36-62	De Rescriptis.
VIII.	Canones 63-79	De Privilegiis.
IX.	Canones 80-86	De Dispensationibus.
X.	Canones 87-107	Generales Notiones de Personis.
XI.	Canones 111-117	De Clericorum Adscriptione Alicui Dioecesi.
XII.	Canones 118-123	De Juribus et Privilegiis Clericorum.
XIII.	Canones 124-144	De Obligationibus Clericorum.
XIV.	Canones 145-195	De Officiis Ecclesiasticis.
XV.	Canones 196-210	De Potestate Ordinaria et Delegata.
XVI.	Canones 211-214	De Reductione Clericorum ad Statum Laicalem.
XVII.	Canones 487-498	De Notione Religionis, et de Erectione et Suppressione Religionis, Provinciae, Domus.
XVIII.	Canones 499-537	De Religionum Regimine.
XIX.	Canones 538-586	De Admissione in Religionem.
XX.	Canones 587-591	De Ratione Studiorum in Religionibus Clericalibus.
XXI.	Canones 592-631	De Obligationibus et Privilegiis Religiosorum.
XXII.	Canones 632-672	De Transitu ad Aliam Religionem, de Egressu e Religione, et de Dimissione Religiosorum.
XXIII.	Canones 673-681	De Societatibus sive Virorum sive Mulierum in Communi Viventium sine Votis.
XXIV.	Canones 1012-1018	De Matrimonio in Genere.
XXV.	Canones 1019-1034	De Iis Quae Matrimonii Celebrationi Praemitti Debent.
XXVI.	Canones 1035-1057	De Impedimentis in Genere.

XXVII.	Canones 1058-1066	De Impedimentis Impedientibus.
XXVIII.	Canones 1067-1080	De Impedimentis Dirimentibus.
XXIX.	Canones 1081-1093	De Consensu Matrimoniale.
XXX.	Canones 1552-1568	De Notione Judicii et de Foro Competenti.
XXXI.	Canones 1569-1607	De Variis Tribunalium Gradibus et Speciebus.
XXXII.	Canones 1608-1645	De Disciplina in Tribunalibus Servanda.
XXXIII.	Canones 1646-1666	De Partibus in Causa.
XXXIV.	Canones 1667-1705	De Actionibus et Exceptionibus.
XXXV.	Canones 1706-1725	De Causae Introductione.
XXXVI.	Canones 1726-1746	De Litis Contestatione, de Litis Instantia, et de Interrogationibus Partibus in Judicio Faciendis.
XXXVII.	Canones 1747-1836	De Probationibus.
XXXVIII.	Canones 1837-1857	De Causis Incidentibus.
XXXIX.	Canones 2195-2198	De Natura Delicti Ejusque Divisione.
XL.	Canones 2199-2211	De Imputabilitate Delicti, de Causis Illam Aggravantibus vel Minuentibus, et de Juridicis Delicti Effectibus.
XLI.	Canones 2212-2213	De Conatu Delicti.
XLII.	Canones 2214-2240	De Poenis in Genere.
XLIII.	Canones 2241-2285	De Poenis Medicinalibus seu de Censuris.
XLIV.	Canones 2286-2305	De Poenis Vindicativis.
XLV.	Canones 2306-2313	De Remediis Poenalibus et Poenitentiis.

DE JURE ROMANO

XLVI. The Periods of Roman Law.
XLVII. The Sources of Roman Law.
XLVIII. Personality.
XLIX. Slavery.
L. Citizenship.
LI. Patria Potestas.
LII. Personae in Manu.
LIII. Personae in Mancipio.
LIV. Tutela et Cura.
LV. Ownership.
LVI. De Obligationibus in Genere.
LVII. De Obligationibus Extra-Contractualibus.
LVIII. Furtum.
LIX. Damnum Injuria Datum.
LX. Injuria.

Tituli

Vidit Facultas:

PHILIPPUS BERNARDINI, S.T.D., J.U.D., Decanus.
LUDOVICUS H. MOTRY, S.T.D., J.C.D., a Secretis.
VALENTINUS T. SCHAAF, O.F.M., J.C.D.
FRANCISCUS J. LARDONE, S.T.D., J.U.D.

Vidit Rector Magnificus Universitatis:

JACOBUS HUGO RYAN, Ph.D., S.T.D.

BIOGRAPHICAL NOTE

William A. Ferry was born in Norristown, Pa., April 14, 1903. He attended St. Patrick's School, Norristown; St. Charles' Seminary, Overbrook; and the Catholic University of America, Washington, D. C. He was ordained priest in May, 1929.

www.ingramcontent.com/pod-product-compliance
Lightning Source LLC
LaVergne TN
LVHW041115090826
844660LV00060B/333

* 9 7 8 0 8 1 3 2 2 2 4 8 6 *